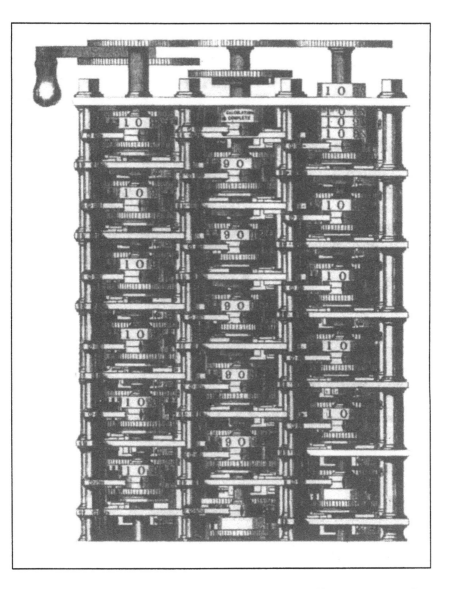

"Impression from a woodcut of a small portion of Mr. Babbage's Difference Engine No. 1."
Frontispiece from *Passages from the Life of a Philosopher*, published in 1864.

T0347482

FRONTISPIECE

TABLE OF CONTENTS

EDITOR'S CORNER

Greetings! Welcome to the new millennium and to a brand-new phase in the life of *Educational Studies*. It seems fitting that this is our first issue with Lawrence Erlbaum Associates as we celebrate our entrance into 2000. We have a sophisticated new cover design and moreover, I am proud to present this Special Issue on Computing and Educational Studies, guest edited by Eugene Provenzo. What better way to usher in this phase than with a focused look on the ways that computers and the Internet are influencing culture and education. I thank Eugene and his students at Miami University, as well as the other contributing authors, Ruthanne Kurth-Schai, Charles R. Green, and Dara H. Wexler, for their hard work getting this issue out to you.

In addition, the American Educational Studies Association (AESA) and the editors of *Educational Studies* acknowledge our gratitude to Dr. Ronald A. Collins, provost at Eastern Michigan University. The support of Dr. Collins enables *Educational Studies* to maintain a home at Eastern Michigan University and Drs. Martusewicz and McCormack to continue to serve as editors of this publication. We are grateful for the opportunity to serve the university and AESA in this capacity. We also appreciate College of Education Dean Jerry Robbins and Department of Teacher Education Head Alane Starko for their continuing support of *Educational Studies*.

With that, I'll just step aside and let the authors and reviewers of this issue take over. Happy New Year! Enjoy!

Rebecca A. Martusewicz
Editor

INTRODUCTION

Special Issue: Computing and Educational Studies

EUGENE F. PROVENZO, JR., Guest Editor
University of Miami

Technology, and more specifically, computing and its impact on education, is a topic that has been largely ignored in the literature in educational studies (the social and cultural foundations of education, educational philosophy, the history of education, education and cultural studies, and the sociology of education). Although there are occasional special presentations and discussions on the subject at the annual meetings of the American Educational Studies Association, Division G of the American Educational Research Association, the Philosophy of Education Society, and the Annual Conference on Curriculum Theory and Classroom Practice (informally known as "Bergamo"), it is clear that, in general, technology and computing are not seen as critically important areas for discussion and analysis. Likewise, the inclusion of technology and educational computing issues in introductory and advanced courses in the social and cultural foundations is limited.

In this special issue of *Educational Studies* we call for a greater awareness of computing as a critical area of study for those interested in educational studies. We argue that computing as a social and curricular issue, although closely linked to topics that are more widely studied in the field (such as race, gender, social class, and literacy), is, in fact, a separate subject of inquiry and is possibly of comparable significance and importance.

We further argue that the general field of educational studies has an obligation to ask a series of critical questions about computing that go far beyond those asked by traditional educational technologists. These are questions that are deeply cultural and social. For example: How important are computers in defining how we function and act as a culture? Why is the micro or personal computer revolution as important as the mainframe revolution? How is it different? Who has benefited most from the computer revolution of the past two decades? Why? How? What are the parallels between the Gutenberg typographic revolution and the recent personal computer revolution? How do computers change the environment for teaching and learning? Who is empowered by computers? Does the computer create new models of power and knowledge? If so, how? Is computing a neutral technology? If not, why? What is the relation between traditional text literacy and computer literacy? What does it mean to be computer literate? What is the cultural significance of computing? Why is the social and cultural meaning of computing so consistently ignored in the education of teachers? The purpose of this special issue of *Educational Studies* is to open up a wider dialogue about computing and education than has previously existed in the field. We argue that the general field of educational studies not only should lay claim to computing and its social, cultural, and curricular meaning as a part of its field but it has an absolute obligation to do so. The field of educational studies might also ask why so few of us have systematically pursued this area of inquiry. If, as many of us in the field would argue, computing and the information revolution are, in fact, the most important educational and cultural issues of this generation, then why have only a handful of scholars in educational studies made computing a focus of their inquiry?

Perhaps it is a generational issue. When I think of social foundations scholars in their forties, fifties, and sixties who have written about technology and educational computing, only a few individuals come to mind: Michael Apple, C. A. Bowers, Bertram C. Bruce, Nicholas Burbules, Tom Callister, Ivor Goodson, Douglas D. Noble, Colin Lankshear, Michael Peters, and me. Anne De Vaney, who has written on a number of aspects of technology and learning, including a book-length analysis of the educational program *Channel One,* has begun to publish a number of articles dealing with the historical and discursive formation of the field of educational technology. Her guest-edited issue of *Theory Into Practice* (1998) is an important collection of articles dealing with questions of technology, media, and to a lesser degree, computing. Her introduction is particularly suggestive in light of the theme for this issue of *Educational Studies.* In many cases, the individuals mentioned here have written occasional articles and book chapters, often in collaboration with others, that are clearly not the main focus of their research and inquiry. (Note: See the references included at the end of "Computing, Culture, and Educational Studies" in this special issue for relevant works.) Among younger social foundations scholars, Hank Bromley is one of the few names that comes immediately to mind. Jeanne M. Connell recently published several articles on technology and education that incorporate a social foundations perspective in *Educational Studies'* sister journal *Educational Foundations.*

In this special issue, we include a piece co-authored by Ruthanne Kurth-Schai, who has articles on technology and education going back at least a decade. We also include an essay by Dara H. Wexler, a newly emerging scholar in the field. These female writers are an exception. Why aren't there more women in the field writing about this subject?

Except for the article by Ruthanne Kurth-Schai and Charles R. Green, "Conversation, Composition, and Courage: Re-envisioning Technologies for Education and Democracy," and Dara H. Wexler's article, "Integrating Computer Technology: Blurring the Roles of Teachers, Students, and Experts," the materials included in this issue emerged from a doctoral seminar (Curriculum History,

Theory, and Computing, 1999) I conducted at the University of Miami. The members of the seminar included Lydia C. Barza, Ellen Emerson Brown, Aubrey Campbell, Michele C. Mits Cash, Lina Lopez Chiappone, Elizabeth D. Cramer, Keith Graziadei, and Philomena Marinaccio.

The books reviewed in this issue represent what the members of the seminar consider a basic selection of some of the key texts in the area. It is by no means a comprehensive selection. Works such as *Beyond the Gutenberg Galaxy: Microcomputers and the Emergence of Post-Typographic Culture* (Provenzo 1986); *Video Kids: Making Sense of Nintendo* (Provenzo 1991); and *Computing, Digital Culture and Pedagogy: the Analytical Engine* (Provenzo n.d.) were not reviewed. Larry Cuban's *Teachers and Machines: The Classroom Use of Technology Since 1920* (1986) was not included, and neither was *Education/Technology/Power: Educational Computing as Social Practice* (Bromley and Apple 1998). In the case of Bromley and Apple's work, the volume just recently came to our attention. Relevant works by Colin Lankshear and Peter McLaren are not included, because they tend to stand more as chapters or sections in books. This is not to ignore their importance but to simply say that we made choices about what we were interested in and felt were important to include in this issue.

What we did do was attempt to review many of the books written in the last ten to fifteen years that we felt were particularly relevant to understanding the social and cultural dimensions of computing for the field of education, and more specifically, educational studies. For those interested in a more comprehensive list of books and articles, please refer to the general list of references after "Computing, Culture, and Educational Studies" in this issue. We hope that the questions raised in this issue provide the basis for a lively discussion and analysis of the place of "Educational Studies" in interpreting the role of computing in our culture and in our educational system. We also hope to provide in future issues of the journal a model for exploring other topics of similar significance and importance to the field. Finally, special thanks to Asterie Baker Provenzo, whose keen editorial skills and insights helped make this special issue of the journal come together.

ARTICLES

Computing, Culture, and Educational Studies

EUGENE F. PROVENZO, JR.
University of Miami

> Any technology tends to create a new human environment.
>
> —*Marshall McLuhan*

Much of the change that has taken place in American education and culture since the late 1960s has been driven by the rapid evolution of media such as television and film, and in particular, the computer. Together, they have created a new cultural geography — what some have referred to as a "virtual geography" (Critical Art Ensemble 1994, 3).

What we have experienced is unprecedented—perhaps the only parallel being the introduction of moveable type and modern printing during the late medieval and early Renaissance period (Provenzo 1986). Like the Gutenberg revolution, the contemporary computer revolution represents a cultural divide in which traditional models of knowledge, communication and learning have been transformed as a result of new forms of media and information transfer. Increasingly, these systems are based on, or heavily dependent on, some form of computing.

This process, whose origins can be traced back to the mainframe computing revolution of the 1950s and 1960s, accelerated with the massive introduction of cheap and affordable computers in the late 1970s. It continued during the 1980s with the growth of computer-based multimedia systems and in the 1990s with the use of the Internet and the World Wide Web.

Although the widespread use of computing is relatively recent, its potential for transforming knowledge and learning has been understood for over sixty years. In 1945, for example, Vannevar Bush (1890–1974), president of the Massachusetts Institute of Technology (MIT), an early computer designer and a key science advisor to President Franklin D. Roosevelt, described a publishing system called a "Memex" (Bush 1945). According to Bush, the Memex would be "a sort of mechanized private file and library … a device in which an individual stores his books, records and communications, and which is mechanized so that it may be consulted with exceeding speed and flexibility. It is an enlarged intimate supplement to his memory" (Nyce and Kahn 1991, 102).

The Memex would be a desk-size device. It would store massive amounts of microfilm so that "if the user inserted 5000 pages of material a day it would take him hundreds of years to fill the repository" (Nyce and Kahn 1991, 102). Most of the content of the Memex could be purchased on microfilm, ready for insertion into the machine. Books, pictures, periodicals, and newspapers could be dropped into the system. Personal notes and materials could be entered as well. An index would be included that would allow the user easy navigation through the system: "A special button transfers him immediately to the first page of the index. Any given book of his library can thus be called up and consulted with far greater facility than if it were taken from a shelf. As he has several projection positions, he can leave one item in position while he calls up another" (103). Marginal notes could be added using a dry photography method (103).

The Memex was totally impractical. Bush's dream of a mechanical device that would allow the individual the means by which to do "associative indexing" includes not only the basic elements of a Web Browser— bookmarks and hypertext (the "combination of blocks of text joined by electronic links"; Landow 1989, 39)—but also a "Windows" screen format (multiple screens that the user can easily move between).

Theorists other than Bush anticipated how computers would look and function. In 1963 for example, Douglas Engelbart, who was then working at the Stanford Research Institute, published "A Conceptual Framework for the Augmentation of Man's Intellect" (Engelbart 1963). In this essay, he outlined not only the basic principles of word processing but also the use of icon systems for computers as well as technologies such as the computer mouse and scanning.

It would take several decades for Engelbart's ideas to be fully implemented. On a cultural level, at about the same time Engelbart was doing his work, the Canadian media theorist Marshall McLuhan was beginning to anticipate some of the profound cultural and technical shifts that were going to affect us as a result of the growth of new forms of media. McLuhan clearly understood that we were at the beginning of a new era. Writing in 1964 in *Understanding Media,* McLuhan explained, "We are today as far into the electric age as the Elizabethans had advanced into the typological and mechanical age. And we are experiencing the same confusions and indecisions which they had felt when living simultaneously in two contrasted forms of society and experience. Whereas the Elizabethans were poised between medieval corporate experience and modern individualism, we reverse their pattern by confronting an electric technology which would seem to render individualism obsolete and the corporate interdependence mandatory" (McLuhan 1964, iv).

McLuhan's most well known concept, the idea of a "Global Village" (a worldwide network of shared information and knowledge) is, in fact, becoming a reality as a result of economic and media globalization and new technologies such as the

Internet and World Wide Web. McLuhan realized that the changes that were being created by these new technologies were not neutral but value laden representing "active processes that reshape people and other technologies alike" (iv).

McLuhan clearly anticipated many of the conditions of postmodernism. The idea of postmodernism would be given a name in the late 1970s by the French cultural theorist Jean-Francois Lyotard. In *La Condition Postmoderne: Rapport Sur le Savoir,* Lyotard argued that Western culture had entered a postmodern period in which traditional narratives of science and culture had been redefined (Lyotard, 1979). Specifically describing knowledge in computerized societies, Lyotard argued that the status of knowledge had been altered as we entered the postmodern era (138).

If this is indeed the case, then the transformation that has occurred in our culture and in our educational system is of profound importance. We are at a watershed, not unlike the dividing line between the oral culture of the late medieval period and the typographic and book-based culture of the early Renaissance. A new literacy is coming into place—one based on new computer-based technologies.

And if this argument is true, then the field of educational studies and the social foundations of education, in general, should be profoundly concerned with questions related to the impact of technology, and more specifically, computing, on our educational system and culture.

And yet, as mentioned in the introduction to this special issue of *Educational Studies,* there has been little discussion of technology and computing as a foundational issue. In the 1980s and early 1990s, only a few books and articles were written by scholars in the social foundations of education that dealt with technology and computing. Most were ignored. Works such as *Beyond the Gutenberg Galaxy: Microcomputers and the Emergence of Post-Typographic Culture* (Provenzo 1986) elicited significant interest in the computing community as well as specialized academic fields such as English composition. Likewise *Video Kids: Making Sense of Nintendo* (Provenzo 1991), which dealt with racism, gender discrimination, and violence in video games, gained worldwide attention with reviews in the *New York Times,* the *London Economist,* and testimony based on the book before the United States Senate. Yet almost no discussion of these books is found in the social foundations literature.

The more significant work of C. A. Bowers, perhaps the most important critic of educational computing in the last two decades, has largely been ignored. Bowers, for example, in his seminal 1988 work, *The Cultural Dimensions of Educational Computing,* questioned, in reference to educational computing, whether or not the computer is a neutral technology. According to him, "The most fundamental question about the new technology has never been seriously raised by either the vocal advocates or the teachers who have attempted to articulate their reservations. The question has to do with whether the technology is neutral; that is, neutral in terms of accurately representing, at the level of the software program, the domains of the real world in which people live" (Bowers 1988, 24).

Bowers argued that computers and their software must be understood as "part of the much more complex symbolic world that makes up our culture"(24). According to him, we need to critically reframe how we look at computers and how they function. Instead of simply understanding them in a technical and procedural context, we need to deal with them in a larger cultural context—how they mediate and change our systems of knowledge and ways of interpreting the world around us (24).

As someone who professionally bridges the two distinct fields of educational computing and the social foundations of education, it is clear to me that the important cultural and social questions of the type being asked by Bowers are largely being ignored by the traditional educational technologists. Most of these people come from fields like educational media, methods, and curriculum. Few have extensive training in social and cultural issues. As reflected in the content of journals such as the *Computing Teacher, Computers in the Schools, Electronic Learning, Educational Technology,* the *Journal of Educational Computing Research,* the *T.H.E. Journal: Technological Horizons in Education,* or standard textbooks like *Educational Computing Foundations* (Simonson and Thompson 1990), *Computer Education for Teachers* (Sharp 1993), *Microcomputers for Twenty-First Century Educators* (Lockard, Abrams, and Many 1994), there is almost no discussion of social and cultural issues involving computing. In the rare instances when there are references to social and cultural issues, they certainly do not reflect the most advanced thinking in either educational studies, or even in the general field of computing. In the bibliographies of the textbooks mentioned, for example, one finds almost none of the books cited in the reference section of this article or the books reviewed in this special issue of *Educational Studies.*

This is not to say that the work of these people is not valuable, but instead to demonstrate that it largely ignores the cultural, social, and educational meaning of technology and computing. Educational computing as a field is very young—basically it came into existence in the late 1970s as a result of the introduction of inexpensive micro or personal computers. People who entered the field came from a variety of disciplines, mostly educational media, or some specialized methods area such as science or mathematics.

Early courses in the field focused on programming, the mechanics of how computers worked, and the use of very limited curriculum models. All of this work was dictated by the newness of the field and the limited computational power of the machines that were being used.

As micro and personal computers, along with their software, became more powerful and flexible by the mid-1980s, the nature of educational computing began to change. More and more, people began to question which models of instruction were most effective on the computer and how these machines and their accompanying software could be most effectively integrated into instruction.

Yet with perhaps the exception of special education, where there was a growing awareness during the 1980s that computers could be adapted to the needs of special populations, there was relatively little discussion in the educational computing community about the social and cultural significance of the use of this new technology. Looking at the titles of selected issues of the main educational computing journals during this period is revealing. Topics focus on subjects such as classroom teaching strategies, new types of software, the use of multimedia, and the implementation of instructional models such as distance education. There are almost no articles that deal with topics such as computers and race, the implied ideology of interface systems, the corporate promotion of educational computing, gender and class issues, and so on.

This is perhaps understandable. As argued earlier, the people who founded the field came almost entirely from specialties that ignored foundational issues such as race, gender, and class. Also, methods of critical social inquiry, which are fundamental to the social foundations and educational studies, are not emphasized.

Yet even among the few authors in the social foundations who have written about computing and education, their analysis in the context of critical pedagogy and theory is extremely limited. In the essay "Critical Pedagogy and Cyberspace" (Lankshear, Peters, and Knoebel 1996), the authors argued that the use of critical pedagogical methods is possible in the context of computing. In a forthcoming book, *Computing, Digital Culture and Pedagogy: The Analytical Engine* (n.d.), I make the same argument and use Jurgen Habermas's "theory of communicative action" and the idea of creating "an ideal speech situation" as a means of interrogating our current use of computers in an education context. Similarly, *Education/Technology/Power* (Bromley and Apple 1998) begins to address this area. In sum, there is very little linking of critical pedagogy to the computing field. In the case of Bowers, I assume he is connecting to somewhat different traditions of inquiry—ones more closely linked to the social and cultural ecology literature.

The general failure to establish social and cultural issues as a major component of training teachers in the use of computers unfortunately leads to their uncritical use. This is extremely problematic because as Bowers pointed out, computers, and their use in educational settings, are hardly a neutral technology.

In fact, there has been a tendency on the part of educators, because of a lack of emphasis on the social and cultural issues, to treat educational technology and computing as an automatic good rather than as a value-laden technology. As a result, the promotion of educational computing takes on almost utopian and messianic qualities. Computing will reinvent the educational system, change the very nature of instruction, and so on. Although this might be true, it probably is not true, and certainly it is not this simple. What is clear is that the question that is largely ignored is "To what effect?"

In this context, commenting on computers in general, MIT professor Joseph Weizenbaum explains: "Yes, the computer did arrive 'just in time.' But in time for what? In time to save—and save very nearly intact, indeed, to entrench and stabilize— social and political structures that otherwise might have been either radically renovated or allowed to totter under the demands that were sure to be made on them. The computer, then, was used to conserve America's social and political institutions. It buttressed them and immunized them, at least temporarily, against enormous pressures for change" (Weizenbaum 1976, 31).

Similarly, Terry Winograd and Fernado Flores questioned what the computer does in the context of human practice (Winograd and Flores 1987, 4).

In the introduction to a previously cited collection of essays, Hank Bromley made the interesting point that the computer has become a "symbol" around which people can rally to promote different educational causes (Bromley 1998, 1–2). On the surface, educational computing can draw people together without their realizing that their goals may be very different. As Bromley explained, "What unites them is the deployment of a shared symbol more than shared interests of a shared vision of the future" (2).

In my experience with local schools, I have seen groups of teachers pursue funding for computers as part of a schoolwide effort because they saw it opening up greater access to knowledge and information for their students, whereas administrators in the same school saw the new technology as providing an opportunity to carefully regulate and track the work of students and teachers using programmed instruction systems. On the surface, both are working for a common purpose, that is, the increased use of computing in the classroom, but each group with a very different end point in mind.

Situations like the one just described suggest that we need to ask much more subtle questions about computing and its use in the schools than have shown up in the literature until this time. Software is rarely analyzed in terms of its ideological or political values. Ann De Vaney pointed out that seemingly neutral and harmless programs like Broderbund Corporation's *Where in the World Is Carmen San Diego* have not so subtle biases in terms of race. Why is it, she asked, that when visitors go to any of the thirty worldwide cities included in the program, they only see White faces? As De Vaney explained:

> Since these are modern products, teachers should ask themselves, not only how do these products position their students but just whom are they inviting into their classroom. If they invite Carmen San Diego, teachers sanction the presence of a stereotypic Hollywood Latino "dark lady," mysterious, curvaceous, and elusive. Alternatively, videos and software must not only picture girls and children of color but provide respectful representations of diverse groups. If in

a video a credible Muslim boy is presented with respect and given agency, there would then be room for the formation of a new subjectivity in the classroom. Knowledge about subjectivity allows a teacher to resist subtly stereotypic constructions as well as to recognize when equitable representations and those with agency come along. (De Vaney 1998a, 74)

The types of issues raised by De Vaney also appear in educational simulation programs. What, for example, is the effect of using educational simulation programs like *The Oregon Trail, Populous,* and *SimCity*? These programs are highly popular—historically some of the best selling titles in educational software. But like every simulation, they have a specific point of view—a particular way of looking at the world.

Populous has been widely used in schools for over a decade. In the program you assume the role of one of two gods who rule a world and its people. One of the gods is evil and the other is good. Each god is assigned a population of people whom they nurture and try to help flourish.

The point of view provided in *Populous* is of an omniscient god who shapes and directs the lives of the people (called "walkers") on the planet. A review of the game published shortly after it was first introduced to the public explained: "Skeptics will be surprised at how enjoyable playing a god turns out to be. The walkers, both good and bad, are fascinating to watch as they move about. They really seem to have lives of their own, and your control over their lives gives you an undeniable sense of power. ... Soon you'll find yourself feeling parental about your followers, nurturing them and watching them grow. You'll be happy to wipe out the evil walkers with volcanoes, swamps, and earthquakes should they stand in the way of your chosen people" (Firme 1990, 36).

What is clearly at work in this simulation is a series of assumptions about the desirability of power and control and about the need of other people to be directed. The viewpoint is that of a powerful god who acts on people (walkers) rather than with people. The world is shaped and defined by a relatively narrow and circumscribed set of forces (volcanoes, earthquakes, etc.).

A simulation such as *Populous* is neither neutral nor without a specific point of view. As Andrew Firme noted, "It's amazingly easy to develop delusions of grandeur while playing *Populous*" (Firme 1990, 90). As foundations scholars we might ask, Will children playing games such as *Populous* simply assume that this is how the world is run? Will they incorporate such models into their own lives? Does a teacher using such a system in the classroom have any means by which to distinguish good from evil, to delineate variables that may be affecting what is occurring in the simulation? How does the omniscient perspective influence what the players do? Would they act differently if they were one of the walkers?

Concerns about the use of a simulation such as *Populous* directly address C. A. Bowers's question of whether "the current state of computer technology used in the classroom strengthens those cultural orientations contributing to a technicist social order and weakens others that cannot be integrated into the new emerging order" (Bowers 1988, 6). In the end, it is clear that the use of simulations is neither neutral nor problem free. It should also be noted that as increasingly sophisticated simulations are created using technologies such as virtual reality, the power of these simulations over the user has the potential to become even greater.

C. A. Bowers, in the forthcoming *Let Them Eat Data: The Ecological and Educational Consequences of Globalizing Computer Cultures* (n.d.), talks at length about the limitations of simulations such as *The Oregon Trail* and the *SimCity* series (*SimCity, SimEarth,* and *SimLife*). His concerns parallel my own about programs like *Populous*. What, for example, is the educational significance of the following description included in the handbook for *SimLife*?

> *SimLife* is the first genetic engineering game available for personal computers. It lets players manipulate the very fabric of existence, giving life to creatures that defy the wildest imaginations. Players create exotic plants and animals of various shapes, sizes, and temperaments, and turn them loose into a custom-designed environment in which only the best adapted species survive! With *SimLife,* the budding mad scientist can people the landscape with mutagens (agents that cause mutation and, indirectly, evolution). Or change the individual genes of one creature and see what effects its offspring have on the long-term survival of its species, and the ecosystem as a whole. (Maxis 1995)

Underlying *SimLife* is the assumption that genetic manipulation is a perfectly normal thing for people to experiment with. There is no question that this may not be something we want to encourage children—some of whom will undoubtedly pursue scientific careers—to do.

Why aren't issues like this being more widely discussed as part of the literature in educational studies? Why aren't issues of race and gender being included as well? In *Video Kids: Making Sense of Nintendo* (Provenzo 1991), I looked at the social content of video games on the Nintendo system, in other words, at the messages conveyed through the main themes of the games. Common themes included rescue, revenge, and the conflict between good and evil. Although my research focused exclusively on the games included in the Nintendo system, my findings applied to video games in general.

I discovered that when women were included in the games on the Nintendo system, they were usually portrayed as persons who were acted *upon* rather than being initiators of actions. In the most extreme and disturbing cases, they were depicted as victims. This fact had important consequences not only for girls but also for boys, who learned from the games that women are the weaker sex and are constantly in need of assistance. The games not only socialized girls to be dependent but also conditioned boys to assume dominant gender roles.

When I interviewed parents and teachers about violence and gender bias in the games, none of them had a very clear idea of what the actual content of the games was. In *Double Dragon II,* the hero, Billy Lee, and his former rival, Jimmy Lee, try to save Billy's girlfriend, Marian, who has been kidnapped by the Black Shadow Warriors. The cover of the game box shows Marian clutching Billy as he supports her with his hand wrapped around the small of her back. His other arm is entwined with a whip that he is wresting out of the hands of a woman who has enormous breasts and a punk Mohawk hairdo. Marian wears a torn mini-dress that reveals curvaceous thighs and buttocks; her tank top is ripped, allowing a glimpse of her midriff and breasts pressed against Billy's chest. With her blonde hair cascading behind her, Marian's face radiates confidence as she is held in the arms of her savior/hero Billy.

The covers on the forty-seven most popular video games in the Nintendo system that were the subject of my research portrayed a total of 115 male and 9 female characters—a ratio of thirteen to one. Twenty of the males strike a dominant pose. None of the females do. Three females (one-third of the total) are shown in submissive circumstances—being kidnapped, carried off, or cowering behind a man. None of the males are depicted as being submissive. Thirteen of the forty-seven games were based on scenarios in which women were kidnapped or rescued as part of the game. These figures are even more significant if we note that nine out of ten of the most popular games had, as their primary theme, women as victims who needed to be rescued. Equally noteworthy was that in all of the games I studied, no man was ever rescued.

Particularly interesting in light of these findings was the fact that in interviewing elementary-age girls about video games, I found that they were intensely interested in playing them but did not like the content of the games that were available. If, as companies like Nintendo have argued (and I believe rightly so), video games are the first introduction of children to the culture of computing, then the initial introduction of girls to computing through video games is highly sexist and limiting. Recent efforts to develop nonsexist games by industry leaders such as Brenda Laurel have largely failed despite an obvious need for such materials.

Many of my colleagues, both inside and outside of the social foundations, have questioned my interest in video games and the socialization of children. Is this an appropriate topic for a serious scholar? Several psychologists have told me that although they found my research on video games interesting, it "wasn't really psychology." But of course, that is just my point. Video games and their role in the construction of children and of gender, race, and culture, are social foundations issues.

Those of us in the social foundations of education who are interested in approaches like critical theory, educational philosophy, educational anthropology, and cultural studies would certainly argue that our research has every reason to be concerned with how children construct their perspectives on culture. It seems clear to me, for example, that the disciplinary areas and methods used by people in the social foundations of education could contribute significantly to helping us understand school shootings like the one in Littleton, Colorado, on April 20, 1999, that led to the suicide of the two killers, the death of a teacher and twelve students, and the wounding of twenty-three others. Within the context of the role of media violence in the construction of childhood and adolescent culture, "first person shooter" computer games and their role in educating players in stylized models of violence are examples of why we should be looking beyond traditional educational computing as a social foundations issue.

Think of Littleton, and then ask yourself, What are the stories American society tells its children? Where do they learn these stories? The great majority are told in different forms of media ranging from television and film, to rock music and computer or video games. Overwhelmingly, these stories are violent. In particular, with film and television, and increasingly with computer games, "technology has transformed violence into a spectacle of stunning beauty" (McLaren and Morris 1997, 115). As McLaren and Morris explained:

> Violence when it's stylized, when it's choreographed and hyperaccelerated or played in slow motion, when it is set to the strains of a poignant Beethoven sonata, the minimalist pulses of a Philip Glass creation, or the tremulous strains and corrosive screams of a Diamanada Galas vocal, can be thrillingly sublime and breathtakingly beautiful. Since the advent of cinema and television, we've been blessed with endless variations: severed heads floating through the air in all the splendor only freeze-frame decapitation can convey; severed arms gliding down elevator shafts while still pulsing arcs of blood; hideously dislocated jaws and cheekbones shattering beyond recognition; noses crumbling like beer cans; eyes gouged by lightening-swift fingers trained by Shaolin priests; skin ceremoniously flayed, revealing as the victim screams, shiny bone laced with blood vessels; intestines greedily gobbled up by lip smacking zombies who look like your Uncle Roger after a night out on the town; mutants giving birth to talking heads; and aliens thrusting about chest cavities like restless adolescents trapped in a small town, finally shooting through their jagged rib cages, snarling giddily past their first few gulps of oxygen. (115)

Narratives of the type described by McLaren and Morris are common in the programs and particularly in movies and games viewed by children and teenagers. Through their emphasis on Baudrillard's (1988) notion of the hyperreal, they distort reality through a trivialization of violence and the effects it has upon us as human beings.

The fact that hyperreal violence of this sort encourages children and adolescents to assume a rhetorical stance that equates violence with style and personal empowerment is an example of another of the types of computer related topics that we should be concerned with as researchers in the social foundations of education.

There are probably dozens of additional topics on the meaning of computing and culture that are worth considering in the field of educational studies: How does computing redefine power and authority in universities and colleges and at the kindergarten through twelfth-grade level? What is the meaning of literacy in a post-typographic or postmodern culture? What are the ethical issues implicit in using computers to augment or enhance intelligence? Who should have access to computing in educational settings? In what forms?

These are just a few of the types of questions we should be asking about computing within educational studies. Most of them are questions that for political reasons, or because of a lack of methodological and theoretical background and training, educational technologists and others in the field of computers and education are not addressing.

These are questions that we, as a field, are uniquely suited to address. They are also among the most important questions facing American education and culture.

References

In addition to providing a general set of references for this article, the following expanded bibliography is intended to provide a working set of references for those interested in pursuing the issue of educational computing and technology as a social and cultural issue.

Ambron, Sueann, and Kristina Hooper, eds. 1988. *Interactive Multimedia: Visions of Multimedia for Developers, Educators, and Information Providers*. Redmond, Wash.: Microsoft Press.

Barrett, Edward. 1988. *Text, ConText, and Hypertext: Writing with and for the Computer*. Cambridge: MIT Press.

Baudrillard, Jean. 1983. *Simulations*. Translated by Paul Foos, Paul Patton, and Phillip Beitchman. New York: Semiotext(e).

———. 1988. *Selected Writings*. Edited by Mark Poster. Stanford, Calif.: Stanford University Press.

Benedikt, Michael. 1992. *Cyberspace: First Steps*. Cambridge: MIT Press.

Beniger, James R. 1986. *The Control Revolution: Technological and Economic Origins of the Information Society*. Cambridge: Harvard University Press.

Birkerts, Sven. 1994. *The Gutenberg Elegies: The Fate of Reading in an Electronic Age*. Boston: Faber and Faber.

Bolter, Jay David. 1984. *Turing's Man: Western Culture in the Computer Age*. Chapel Hill: University of North Carolina Press.

———. 1991. *Writing Space: The Computer, Hypertext, and the History of Writing*. Hillsdale, N.J.: Lawrence Erlbaum Associates, Inc.

Bowers, C. A. 1988. *The Cultural Dimensions of Educational Computing: Understanding the Non-Neutrality of Technology*. New York: Teachers College Press.

———. 1995. *Educating for an Ecologically Sustainable Culture: Rethinking Moral Education, Creativity, Intelligence and Other Modern Orthodoxies*. Albany: State University of New York Press.

————. n.d. *Let Them Eat Data: The Ecological and Educational Consequences of Globalizing Computer Cultures.* Athens: University of Georgia Press, in press.

Brand, Stewart. 1988. *The Media Lab: Inventing the Future at M.I.T.* New York: Penguin.

Brett, Arlene, and Eugene F. Provenzo, Jr. 1995. *Adaptive Technology for Special Human Needs.* Albany: State University of New York Press.

Bromley, Hank. 1998. "Introduction: Data-Driven Democracy? Social Assessment of Educational Computing." Pp. 1–25 in *Education/Technology/Power: Educational Computing as Social Practice.* Edited by Hank Bromley and Michael W. Apple. New York: State University of New York Press.

Bruce, Bertram C. 1996. "Technology as Social Practice." *Educational Foundations* 10(4): 51–58.

Burbules, Nicholas C. 1996. "Technology and Changing Educational Communities." *Educational Foundations* 10(4): 21–32.

Burbules, Nicholas C., and Bertram C. Bruce. 1995. "This Is Not a Paper." *Educational Researcher* 24(8): 12–18.

Burbules, Nicholas C., and Thomas Callister. 1996. "Knowledge at the Crossroads: Some Alternative Futures of Hypertext Learning Environments." *Educational Theory* 46 (Winter): 23.

Bush, Vannevar. 1945. "As We May Think." *Atlantic Monthly* 176(1): 101–108.

Butler, Samuel. 1967. *Erewhon.* New York: Airmont.

Chaiklin, Seth, and Matthew W. Lewis. 1988. "Will There Be Teachers in the Classroom of the Future? ... But We Don't Think about That." *Teachers College Record* 89(3): 431–440.

Connell, Jeanne M. 1996. "Exploring Some of the Educational Implications of Ihde's Philosophy of Technology." *Educational Foundations* 10(4): 5–12.

Conklin, Jeff. 1987. "Hypertext: An Introduction and Survey." *Computer* 20(9): 17–41.

Critical Art Ensemble. 1994. *The Electronic Disturbance.* New York: Automedia.

Cuban, Larry. 1986.*Teachers and Machines: The Classroom Use of Technology Since 1920.* New York: Teachers College Press.

Delany, Paul, and George P. Landow, eds. 1991. *Hypermedia and Literary Studies.* Cambridge: MIT Press.

Dede, Christopher J. 1987. "Empowering Environments, Hypermedia and Microworlds." *The Computing Teacher* (November): 20–24, 61.

De Vaney, Ann. 1998a. "Can and Need Educational Technology Become a Postmodern Enterprise?" *Theory into Practice* (Winter): 72–81, 37.

————. 1998b. "Will Educators Ever Unmask That Determiner Technology?" *Educational Policy* (September): 568–585, 12.

Drexler, Eric. 1986. *Engines of Creation.* New York: Doubleday.

Ecco, Umberto. 1990. *Travels in Hyperreality.* Translated by William Weaver. New York: Harcourt Brace.

Eisenstein, Elizabeth. 1983. *The Printing Revolution in Early Modern Europe.* New York: Cambridge University Press.

————. 1986. *Print Culture and Enlightenment Thought.* Chapel Hill, N.C.: Hanes Foundation.

Englebart, Douglas.1963. "A Conceptual Framework for the Augmentation of Man's Intellect." Pp. 1–29 in *Vistas in Information Handling.* Edited by P. W. Howerton and D. C. Weeks. Vol. 1, *The Augmentation of Man's Intellect by Machine.* Washington, D.C.: Spartan Books.

Firme, Matthew A. 1990. "Populous." *Game Player's PC Strategy Guide* (March/April).

Gibson, William. 1984. *Neuromancer.* New York: Ace.

Goodson, Ivor F., and Marshall J. Mangan. 1995. "Subject Cultures and the Introduction of Classroom Computers." *British Educational Research Journal* 21(5).

Greif, Irene, ed. 1988. *Computer-Supported Cooperative Work: A Book of Readings.* San Mateo, Calif.: Morgan Kaufmann.

Hardison, O. B. 1989. *Disappearing Through the Skylight: Culture and Technology in the Twentieth Century*. New York: Penguin.

Heim, Michael. 1993. *The Metaphysics of Virtual Reality*. New York: Oxford University Press.

Joyce, Michael. 1995. *Of Two Minds: Hypertext Pedagogy and Politics*. Ann Arbor: University of Michigan Press.

Landow, George P. 1989. "The Rhetoric of Hypermedia: Some Rules for Authors." *Journal of Computing in Higher Education* 1(1).

———. 1992. *Hypertext: The Convergence of Contemporary Critical Theory and Technology*. Baltimore: Johns Hopkins University Press.

Lanham, Richard A. 1993. *The Electronic Word: Democracy, Technology and the Arts*. Chicago: University of Chicago Press.

Lankshear, Colin, Michael Peters, and Michele Knoebel. 1996. "Critical Pedagogy and Cyberspace." Pp. 148–149 in *Counternarratives: Cultural Studies and Critical Pedagogies in Postmodern Spaces*. Edited by Henry A. Giroux, Colin Lankshear, Peter McLaren, and Michael Peters. New York: Routledge.

Lévy, Pierre. 1997. *Collective Intelligence: Mankind's Emerging World in Cyberspace*. New York: Plenum Trade.

Levy, Steven. 1984. *Hackers: Heroes of the Computer Revolution*. New York: Dell.

———. 1989. "People and Computers in Commerce: A Spreadsheet Way of Knowledge." Pp. 318–326 in *Computers in the Human Context*. Edited by Tom Forester. Cambridge: MIT Press.

Lockard, James, Peter Abrams, and Wesley A. Many. 1994. *Microcomputers for Twenty-First Century Educators*. New York: Harper & Collins College Publishers.

Luke, Timothy W. 1991. "Touring Hyperreality: Critical Theory Confronts Informational Society." Pp. 1–26 in *Critical Theory Now*. Edited by Philip Wexler. London: The Falmer Press.

Lyon, David. 1994. *The Electronic Eye: The Rise of the Surveillance Society*. Minneapolis: The University of Minnesota Press.

Lyotard, Jean-Francois. 1979. *La Condition Postmoderne: Rapport Sur le Savoir*. Paris: Les Editions de Minuit.

———. 1992. "Answering the Question: What Is Postmodernism?" Pp. 138–150 in *The Post-Modern Reader*. Edited by Charles Jencks. New York: St. Martin's Press.

Maxis. 1995. *SimLife*. Orinda, Calif.

McClintock, Robert O. 1988. "Marking the Second Frontier." *Teachers College Record* 89(3) (Spring): 345–351.

McLaren, Peter, and Janet Morris. 1997. "Mighty Morphin Power Rangers: The Aesthetics of Phallo–Militaristic Justice." Pp. 115–127 in *Kinder–Culture: The Corporate Construction of Childhood*. Edited by Shirley R. Steinberg and Joe L. Kincheloe. Boulder, Colo.: Westview Press.

McLuhan, Marshall. 1962. *The Gutenberg Galaxy: The Making of Typographic Man*. Toronto: University of Toronto Press.

———. 1964. *Understanding Media: The Extensions of Man*. New York: Mentor Books.

———. 1994. *Understanding Media: The Extensions of Man*. Thirtieth anniversary edition with a new introduction by Lewis Lapham. Cambridge: MIT Press.

Minsky, Marvin. 1987. *The Society of Mind*. New York: Simon & Schuster.

Moravec, Hans. 1988. *Mind Children: The Future of Robot and Human Intelligence*. Cambridge: Harvard University Press.

Negroponte, Nicholas. 1970. *The Architecture Machine*. Cambridge: MIT Press.

———. 1995. *Being Digital*. New York: Knopf.

Nelson, Theodor Holm. 1967. "Getting It Out of Our System." In *Information Retrieval: A Critical Review*. Edited by G. Schechter. Washington, D.C.: Thompson Books.

———. 1980. "Replacing the Printed Word: A Complete Literary System." Pp. 1013–1023 in *IFIP Proceedings* (October).

―――. 1987. *Dream Machines.* Redmond, Wash.: Microsoft Press.

―――. 1987. *Literary Machines, Edition 87.1 (The Report On, and Of, Project Xanadu Concerning Word Processing, Electronic Publishing, Hypertext, Thinkertoys, Tomorrow's Intellectual Revolution, and Certain Other Topics Including Knowledge, Education and Freedom).* Bellevue, Wash.: Microsoft Press.

Nix, Don. 1988. "Should Computers Know What You Can Do With Them?" *Teachers College Record* 89(3): 418–430.

Noble, Douglas. 1984. "Computer Literacy and Ideology." *Teachers College Record* 85(4): 603–614.

―――. 1991. *The Classroom Arsenal: Military Research, Information Technology, and Public Education.* New York: Falmer.

―――. 1996. "Mad Rushes into the Future: The Overselling of Educational Technology." *Educational Leadership* 54(3): 18, 6p, 2bw.

Nyce, James M., and Paul Kahn, eds. 1991. *From Memex to Hypertext: Vannevar Bush and the Mind's Machine.* Boston: Academic.

Ong, Walter. 1982. *Orality and Literacy: The Technologizing of the Word.* London: Methuen.

Paz, Octavio. 1987. "The New Analogy: Poetry and Technology." Pp. 119–142 in *Convergence: Essays on Art and Literature.* Translated from the Spanish by Helen Lane. San Diego: Harcourt Brace.

Peters, Michael. 1996. "Literacy and Digital Texts." *Educational Theory* 46 (Winter): 51.

Pool, Ithiel de Sola. 1983. *Technologies of Freedom: On Free Speech in an Electronic Age.* Cambridge: Harvard University Press.

Provenzo, Eugene F., Jr. 1986. *Beyond the Gutenberg Galaxy: Microcomputers and the Emergence of Post-Typographic Culture.* New York: Teachers College Press.

―――. 1991. *Video Kids: Making Sense of Nintendo.* Cambridge: Harvard University Press.

―――. 1992. "The Electronic Panopticon: Censorship, Control and Indoctrination in a Post-Typographic Culture." Pp. 167–178 in *Literacy Online: The Promise (and Peril) of Reading and Writing with Computers.* Edited by Myron Tuman. Pittsburgh: University of Pittsburgh Press.

―――. 1997a. "Electronically Mediated and Simulated Playscapes." Pp. 513–518 in *Play from Birth to Twelve: Contexts, Perspectives and Meanings.* Edited by Doris Fromberg and Doris Bergen. New York: Garland.

―――. 1997b. "Video Games and the Emergence of Interactive Media for Children." Pp. 103–113 in *Kinder-Culture: The Corporate Construction of Childhood.* Edited by Shirley R. Steinberg and Joe L. Kincheloe. Boulder, Colo.: Westview Press.

―――. 1998. "Educational Computing as a Value-Laden Technology." Pp. 299–307 in *Critical Social Issues in American Education: Transformation in a Postmodern World.* 2nd ed. Edited by Svi Shapiro and David Purpel. Mahwah, N.J.: Lawrence Erlbaum Associates, Inc.

―――. n.d. *Computing, Digital Culture and Pedagogy: The Analytical Engine.* New York: Peter Lang, in press.

―――. n.d. *Computing, Scholarship and Learning: The Analytical Engine.* Albany: State University of New York Press, in press.

―――. n.d. "Educational Technology and the Discourse of Education and Schooling." In *Power/Knowledge & The Politics of Educational Meaning: A Teacher's Guide.* Edited by David Gabbard. Mahwah, N.J.: Lawrence Erlbaum Associates, Inc., in press.

Provenzo, Eugene F., Jr., Arlene Brett, and Gary McCloskey. 1999. *Computers, Curriculum and Cultural Change: An Introduction for Teachers.* Mahwah, N.J.: Lawrence Erlbaum Associates, Inc.

Seal-Wanner, Carla. 1988. "Interactive Video Systems: Their Promises and Educational Potential." *Teachers College Record* 89(3): 373–383.

Sharp, Vicki. 1993. *Computer Education for Teachers.* Madison, Wisc.: Brown & Benchmark.

Simonson, Michael, and Ann Thompson. 1990. *Educational Computing Foundations.* Columbus, Ohio: Merrill.

Sloan, Douglas. 1984. "On Raising Critical Questions About the Computer and Education." *Teachers College Record* 85(4): 539–547.

Stinchcombe, Arthur L. 1965. "Social Structure and Organizations." Pp. 142–260 in *Handbook of Organizations.* Edited by James G. March. Chicago: Rand McNally.

Talbot, Stephen L. 1995. *The Future Does Not Compute: Transcending the Machines in Our Midst.* Sebastopol: Calif.: O'Reilly & Associates, Inc.

Tuman, Myron C., ed. 1992. *Literacy Online: The Promise (and Peril) of Reading and Writing with Computers.* Pittsburgh: University of Pittsburgh Press.

Turkle, Sherry. 1995. *Life on the Screen: Identity in the Age of the Internet.* New York: Simon & Schuster.

Vinge, Vernor. 1989. *True Names ... and Other Dangers.* New York: Baen Books.

Weizenbaum, Joseph. 1976. *Computer Power and Human Reason.* San Francisco: Freeman.

Wiener, Norbert. 1967. *The Human Use of Human Beings: Cybernetics and Society.* New York: Avon Books.

Wilkins, John. 1968. *An Essay Towards a Real Character and a Philosophical Language.* Edited by R. C. Alston, English Linguistics 1500–1800, no. 119.1668. Reprint, Menston, England: Scolar Press.

Winograd, Terry, and Fernando Flores. 1987. *Understanding Computers and Cognition.* Reading, Mass.: Addison-Wesley.

Zuboff, Shoshana. 1988. *In the Age of the Smart Machine: The Future of Work and Power.* New York: Basic Books.

Correspondence should be addressed to Eugene F. Provenzo, Jr., 4939 Riviera Drive, Coral Gables, FL 33146.

Conversation, Composition, and Courage: Re-envisioning Technologies for Education and Democracy

RUTHANNE KURTH-SCHAI
Macalester College

CHARLES R. GREEN
Macalester College

Two dozen miles from our campus, a complex politics has been enacted over the past half dozen years. The conversations about a proposed bridge across a scenic river, which is also an interstate boundary, has involved government agencies at all levels, interest groups, community organizations, corporations, labor unions, and individual citizens in various types of intense exchanges. Few would characterize the exchanges as "substantive educational experiences," many saw them as a kind of tragic theater, and most heard the familiar sounds of "politics as usual." The politics included the typical elements: institutional positions, uneven resources, competing expertise, multiple experiences, a variety of visions, and a common impatience with the process. At a lengthy community meeting late last summer one tired and frustrated woman said, "Maybe there should have been some of us just plain folks in on all the planning—including being on the bridge design team. After all, isn't this a democracy?" Two highway engineers across the room heard her and rolled their eyes in what seemed like practiced unison.

Two dozen blocks from our campus, an elementary public school teacher sat in front of one of a half dozen classroom computers the week before school began. Although there had been a few of the usual glitches in starting up again and installing new software, he appreciated the access to information technology, all the new machines, and the technical staff assistant who was helping him set up. His frustration was with the difficulty in adapting the software programs to the needs of his classroom and to his own teaching style. He mused out loud, "I'm almost as driven in my teaching by what this software requires as I am by the new programs at school this year or all the state-mandated student performance and graduation requirements. Maybe there should have been some teachers in the group that produced this stuff ... and maybe some student involvement all through the software design and testing!" The technical assistant looked away in disbelief.

The politics, contexts, and implications of these two bridging technologies are not dissimilar. The movement of goods and people and the transportation of ideas and values in a democracy require building many bridges and crossing many boundaries. Important connections among and possibilities for democracy, education, and technology are prominent features of our perennial analytic and advocacy discussions of public education. There are many voices distributed across time–space—some amplified through position or crisis, some muted and barely audible in the background. To whom do we listen? Many criticisms, stories, initiatives, and dreams are expressed. For what are we listening?

In this article we propose that re-envisioning democracy, education, and technology, and their complex linkages, requires *transformative listening* (Bickford 1996; Garrison 1996; Kurth-Schai and Green n.d.). The momentum of the dominant visual metaphor in calling for re-envisionment, although highly generative, could obscure the necessary fuller integration of all the senses in shaping political and educational reform. Just as many views are necessary in accountable educational technology designs and applications, many voices are required to support the teaching and learning necessary to sustain a democracy.

The Voices of Founders and Critics

Throughout our multilayered public education discourse, American thinkers and activists have analyzed, interpreted, and advocated particular relations between democracy, education, and technology. To whom have we listened and what have they told us? From Thomas Jefferson through John Dewey to contemporary commentators, highly problematic consequences, as well as promising possibilities for more just and productive social relations, have been articulated.

Many of the works of Thomas Jefferson reflect on foundational connections between education and democracy and raise at least four issues of continuing interest. First, Jefferson expressed strong advocacy for mass public education. Second, he wrote about the challenges of structuring education to meet both the needs of the individual and the needs of a democratic society. He was particularly emphatic about the role of education in promoting broadly based public writing and its role in fostering thoughtful conversation to sustain and evolve democratic culture and politics. Third, he demonstrated a continuing struggle with deep tensions between his rural and somewhat aristocratic preferences (including his ambivalence over slavery and class) and the emergence of a dynamic urban, commercial, and early industrial social reality with newly incorporated participants and values that he found mostly threatening. Fourth, across much of his writing he touched on the many risks and uncertainties inherent within the democratic adventure (Burstein 1995; Ellis 1998; Lehman 1985; Malone 1948).

Although much of Jefferson's thinking is embedded in and relevant to our current discussions, educational policy discourse is more distinctively shaped by the voice of John Dewey. He provides for us a foundational analysis that identifies major risks as well as important potentials in his advocacy of explicitly democratic approaches to learning and civic life (Dewey 1984). Moving beyond Jefferson's consideration of technology, Dewey proposed that "thinking is technological insofar as it utilizes tools and instruments: some of those tools are conceptual, some physical, some, the hardware that extends our limbs and senses" (Hickman 1990, 36). The intellectual and physical technologies we use in learning, deciding, implementing, and evaluating can shape the articulation of ends and often modify our goals as we proceed. Not only are ends affected by the means employed but "evolving ends demand the modification of existing tools" (202). Because technologies both shape and support processes of inquiry and political advocacy, Dewey asserts that our tools are no more ethically neutral than are plants, nonhuman animals, or human beings themselves. "They are interactive within situations that teem with value" (202). For Dewey, both obvious and subtle interdependencies among humans and their tool systems play significant roles in forming our democratic and educational ambitions. He framed his considerations of the possibilities for democracy, education, and technology in the language of his time—often embedded in the concept of *industrial arts* (Dewey 1984). It may be useful soon to conceptualize "postindustrial arts" and "postmodern arts" as valuable coinages in some contemporary exchanges in our continuous re-envisionment work (Zargori, Partick, and Coddington 1996). If information age talk alerts us to postindustrial realities, and critical deconstructions move us to new interpretations of modernity and its successors, then extending our enriched visions to include opportunities for artfully used technologies seems appropriate.

Contemporary educational commentators and critics help reveal the always unfinished portions of Jefferson's (Ellis 1998) and Dewey's (Festenstein 1997) visions as well as highlight many unproductive and often tragic features of the current interlocked systems of democracy, education, and technology. There is lively reconsideration of democracy's general situation and prospects (Barber 1984; Bickford 1996; Connolly 1991; Lummis 1996; Sandel 1996) and of democracy's integral relations with education (Apple 1993; Barber 1992; Kahne 1996) with an important subset focusing on technological connections (Bowers 1993; Bromley and Apple 1998; Croft 1993-94; Kane 1999; Raboy and Bruk 1989).

These current commentaries also frame our project. We find such analyses sensitive to many forms of hyper-individualism (but perhaps providing an incomplete reading of the strengths and weaknesses of both a rights-centered social/political/economic paradigm and an embedded methodological individualism), persistent on the theme of pervasive consumerism (but perhaps with little ingenuity on ways and means to find alternatives), and attentive to the many constructions of American exceptionalism (but perhaps with some inattention to global resources and opportunities). These critical voices skillfully direct thinking toward the central problems of democratic and education practices in a late twentieth century, postindustrial global capitalism. Our task here is neither to summarize these provocative critiques nor to develop our reservations about some of these lines of analyses. We do, however, acknowledge our connection, note our gratitude for their insights and influence, and state our commitment to the necessity of continuing conversations.

There are also contemporary voices that speak to new opportunities (Burbules 1997; Egan 1997; Lanham 1993; Sclove 1995). Our teaching and learning tools need not be arrayed only as extensions of an individualistic consumer psychology and political economy. Responsible, participatory, and distributed technological development is a demonstrable possibility (Sclove 1995). Recent findings in cognitive science (Norman 1992, 1998; Schrage 1990) and related learning theory research (Callister 1994; Carroll 1997; Palincsar 1998; Schacter, Norman, and Koutstaal 1998) are in important ways continuous with Jefferson and Dewey. Much of this research features the need for continuous adaptation in human–technological interactions and flexible uses of information technologies. One broadly observant interpreter reminds us that we must understand the expressive context of our time as one in which the uses of technology to enhance data visualization and sonification are fundamentally creative acts that are both individual and social (Lanham 1993).

Transformative Listening

Carrying the many voices suggested in the preceding sections—from the voices overheard in the opening vignettes, through the foundational voices of Jefferson and Dewey, to the rich voices of current commentators and critics—there is much challenging listening to do. But to carry these voices and the others they represent, it is necessary to attend to more than the content of their particular stylized words. A specialized form of listening is also required if we are to develop technologies that can support our efforts to transform education and democracy.

We suggest that this form of listening is defined through the complex interactions among five interrelated characteristics. Listening in order to create and sustain experiences of deep learning and democratic living is a radically social, creative, ethical, aesthetic, and exploratory process. Our experience has taught us that learning to listen in this manner can be supported through intensive engagements with specific pedagogies and their supporting technologies that we describe as conversational, compositional, and courageous. We further propose that the technology necessary to support this form of listening currently exists and is reasonably accessible. It is possible to begin the process of transforming education and democracy by first arraying and using available technology differently, then working to sustain the emergence of even more supportive ones.

Let us now take a look at three pedagogical styles with supporting technologies that might be integrated to promote transformative listening.

Conversational Pedagogy and Supporting Technology

Speaking and listening have always been important features of democratic life in schools and communities. In his classic work, *Democracy and Education,* John Dewey defined criteria still useful today for judging the quality of our efforts to promote inclusive, goal-centered conversations and the role of technology in supporting these. Dewey proposed that the quality of a community's ability to learn and to live together is measured by how fully and freely its members interact around numerous, broad, and varied interests (Dewey 1984). He regarded conversation as perhaps the most important method of social interaction (Garrison 1996).

Following Dewey's lead, in an undergraduate educational policy course titled *Re-envisioning Education & Democracy,* we ask our students to grapple with the complex task of orchestrating the collaborative design of an urban middle school centered in the theme of educating for democracy. We begin by posing questions concerning whose voices must be heard. In order to hear each other's voices—and those of middle-school teachers, parents, students, community representatives, policy players, educational researchers, analysts, and activists—we employ technological support in the form of a variation of the Delphi method (Linestone and Turhoff 1975).

Although the Delphi technology originated as a quantitative technique for acquiring expert opinion to produce technological forecasts, its potential to support intensive and broad-based conversations concerning complex issues soon became apparent. Adaptations of the technique for use in a wide range of social settings, including education, demonstrated the utility of the Delphi in supporting policy analysis, design, and evaluation (Cogan and Derricott 1998; Kurth-Schai 1991; Patrina and Volk 1992). Our interest in this technique centers on recent variations developed to support collaborative social inquiry and systems design. These methodological innovations enhance the utility of the Delphi as a social technology capable of assisting members of a community first in developing a shared vision of possible, desirable, and sustainable futures and then in identifying feasible strategies that might be used to enact that vision.

The Delphi process is distinctive as a conversational technique in that it provides opportunities for clarifying and evolving opinion and commitments in a socially interactive setting while carefully protecting personal privacy. Participants are asked to respond anonymously to a carefully developed forced-choice questionnaire over a series of rounds. Because the questionnaire must provide an accurate representation of the complexity and controversy of the issue or task under consideration, varied techniques are used to ensure that diverse resources and perspectives are reflected in its design. Between rounds participants are given statistical summaries of the group's response so that they might reconsider and possibly revise their initial judgments in light of the opinions of others. Response in the form of open-ended commentary is also invited, analyzed, and shared. The process is continued until a predetermined level of agreement regarding key design priorities is reached.

Students enter the complex conversation necessary to support middle-school design by working together to develop a Delphi questionnaire. They explore and interpret contemporary opinion and research embodied in the assigned course reading. Later they incorporate insights gained through carefully prepared interviews with college faculty and middle-school teachers, administrators, and students.

When we read foundational thinkers and current commentators with our students, we encourage a conversational approach to reading in several familiar senses. We urge our students to consider the context that shaped each author's work and advocate author–reader interactions that attempt to go beyond that necessary but insufficient reflex: What does the author mean here? We hope to have students ask, for example, Whose voices and what experiences might have influenced the authors? What silences do the authors leave? What further inferences, generalizations, or other connections might be appropriate? We also have them converse with their colleagues and with us in ways that bring their experiences, perspectives, and their hopes and fears to the surface on and in their own terms.

During the interviewing phase, we encourage students to move beyond a script/list interview format by establishing an informal, interpersonally connective style. This in-course conversation is broadened and deepened as students assume responsibility for drawing out, clarifying, and eventually providing responsible representations of and advocacy for others whose are voices are often quite different from their own.

Perhaps the most significant conversational challenge is that of negotiating the content and wording of the statements that will appear on the final Delphi questionnaire. Over a period of several weeks, the students work intensively together in small groups to revise, combine, eliminate, and prioritize possible statements. This process continues until the range of issues and voices raised are responsibly reflected in a series of clearly worded, reader-friendly response items. From the hundreds of insights gained through careful consideration of the readings, interviews, and personal preferences, approximately fifty are included in the questionnaire to which the interviewees, course members, and other targeted individuals respond.

This initial phase of the design conversation culminates as questionnaire results are tabulated and shared. Statements most frequently selected as highest priority recommendations can then be used to guide the middle-school design. These ranked preferences provide both an initial glimpse of the Delphi respondents' shared vision and a means through which our course members are held accountable to their varied constituents as they move on with their design tasks.

Through our engagement with the Delphi technology, we work at developing with our students a practiced sense of the radically social and ethical character of listening. The central intention is to discover meaningful and surprising connections across many and varied perspectives. A glimpse of this style at its best would demonstrate the nonhierarchical, interactive, expressively developed inquiry features required to refine the art of compromise and to revitalize contemporary democratic practice.

Although the sharing of diverse and at times controversial positions is best initiated and sustained within the context of trusting and respectful interpersonal relationships, information processing technologies can play a significant supporting role. Now, more than ever before, we need to develop skills in processing and prioritizing diverse and extensive sources of information. Given appropriate technological support, large numbers of ideas can be gathered, disseminated, integrated, synthesized, and interpreted in dynamic and interconnected ways. Information technologies can also be arrayed to address ethical concerns. By separating specific opinions and recommendations from their source at key points in social planning and decision-making processes, we strengthen our efforts to protect privacy and confidentiality while encouraging full participation regardless of social status (e.g., socioeconomic class, race, gender, age, or level of expertise). In each of these ways, full and free interaction around diverse issues and interests can be extended and enhanced.

Compositional Pedagogy and Supporting Technology

Students and teachers are always composing. Our traditional emphasis on the individually written composition with its appropriate literary forms can obscure the potential for collaborative composition and the central role of listening. If we are successful in becoming more inclusive in our conversational inquiries—as we turn to composition—we will need to know what we should listen for.

The word *composition* implies not only the inclusion of carefully selected elements but also their creative arrangement in an aesthetically pleasing manner. Beyond the ability to hear and to respectfully incorporate diverse voices in social inquiry and systems design is the capacity to listen artistically for those very special connections that integrate purpose and beauty into an inspirational whole. This is significant because it is the inspirational quality of a communal vision that guides and motivates imaginative attempts to translate shared dreams into educational and democratic realities.

For our students, the results of the Delphi questionnaire are informative but not typically inspirational. There is a tendency to interpret design priorities in a manner that constrains ethical and pragmatic response rather than opening new possibilities for principled thought and action. There is a risk of narrowing in on surface understandings of the mean or the majority opinion and then settling for the safety of familiar solution paths. Further support is needed to develop the aesthetic and creative dimensions of transformative listening.

The lives of middle-school students provide perhaps the most moving source of inspiration for middle school design. A variety of techniques are used to support the quality of listening necessary to gain insight into the social, emotional, physical, and intellectual worlds of urban youth. Throughout the semester, service learning projects are used to ensure regular interaction with young adolescents. Upon completion of the Delphi, we ask our students to integrate on-site experiences with recollections of their own middle-school years and contemporary research findings into a narrative account written from the point of view of a middle-school student. A relevant symbolic expression (music, poetry, visual imagery) is also required. The narratives are submitted on Nicenet (www.nicenet.org)[1] a course documentation and conferencing tool available for use free of charge on the Internet. What results is an on-line collection of pointed vignettes with connections to virtual constituents that can extend interactions and compel design creativity and accountability in ways that even the consensually generated priority statements cannot.

Students carry the voices represented in these individually composed narratives on into the next phase of the design process during which time small groups collaborate on key design tasks. Strategic storytelling supported by www.nicenet.org is used again, this time to push the evolution and integration of specific design features. Group members determine which design components should be explored and then develop for each other narrative projections written from the perspective of individuals (students, teachers, parents, school administrators) experiencing the component in action.

As these stories are woven across continuing design conversations within and among small groups, we move on to the most challenging level of communal composition: the negotiation, arrangement, and presentation of a coherent and compelling middle-school proposal. The proposal is posted on the World Wide Web in the form of an executive summary supported by numerous appendices (elaboration of specific design features, supporting research and bibliographic references, Delphi questionnaire and findings, state curricular guidelines/graduation standards). We also include in the appendices the course members' narratives that form one dimension of the design context.

Compositional processes and possibilities can then be made visible, expanded, and enlivened through use of hypertext and hypermedia software. Engagement with the aesthetics of more conscious linking of standard policy descriptions of school features with the planning narratives, related symbolic expressions, and other external resources and responses can be improved. All who participated in the design process, as well as interested others, are invited to enter an on-line conversation. Through the interchanges that ensue, new opportunities for artistry and accountability can be opened.

In contemporary voices, we hear echoes of Dewey's thoughts suggesting that teacher/learners (and responsible citizens) are moral artists whose work is enhanced by collaborating with others in developing and acting upon an evolving capacity for moral imagination (Garrison 1997; Johnson 1993; O'Riley 1996). Through our engagement with varied forms of compositional technologies, we strive with our students to create opportunities to directly experience and mindfully attend to those connections between power and beauty and between ethics and aesthetics that are capable of transforming our social, political, and educational lives.

Courageous Pedagogy and Supporting Technology

The achievement of an imaginative, accountable composition—a design for an urban middle school—is a moment of pause and silence. Akin to a musical rest, this moment provides a break to contemplate all that has been accomplished and to anticipate what is to come. Whether the outcome is consensus on a blueprint for a new charter school or agreement on a particular set of policy guidelines, this is a crucial juncture in the life of any democratic project. It is at this point that the listening often stops. There is a strong temptation (often for good reason!) to hold tightly to the hard-won consensual vision in it purist form, uncontaminated and uncomplicated either by the chaotic music of new voices or the jarring sounds of democratic ideals colliding with bureaucratic realities.

For the students, upon completion of the middle-school proposal design, the academic semester comes to a close. As they leave the college classroom, we know that many will continue to enact and evolve their commitments to democratic policy and practice as teachers, school administrators, youth workers, community advocates, policy analysts, politicians, and parents. How can we prepare them to continue listening through all that lies ahead?

Just as completion of a democratic design can signal a time for focusing inward both to celebrate achievements and to anticipate the challenges of implementation, it can also be a time to reach out again to gather new perspectives, a time to join together in exploratory listening to the future. However, this is not an easy task. Moving on, from and through conversation and composition requires courage—a courage that is at once individual and social.

To explore is to act creatively within the context of an often unknown and challenging world. Exploration is dependent upon a radical sense of openness—the willingness to seek out and then listen intently to new voices that continually re-open even the most inclusively and artistically composed personal convictions and social visions to further consideration, compromise, and change.

As the process of exploration moves beyond openness to action, we are called upon to live with the complex consequences of engaging in bold constructions of education and democracy. Those who propose new approaches to democratic learning and life quickly find themselves immersed in a myriad of high stakes situations that require experimental and unprecedented responses. Repeatedly, they must summon the courage to persist in the face of uncertainty, ambiguity, felt inadequacy, and pressures to revert to education and politics "as usual."

Experience has taught us that such efforts, though valiant, far too often result in tragic tales of the increasingly isolated and alienated individual or very small group that struggles against all odds to sustain an instantiation of *the* answer within an oppressive, at times openly hostile, environment. Defensive and oppositional political strategies soon prevail, justified by a growing and ultimately paralyzing sense of victimization (Kurth-Schai and Green 1997).

There Must Be Another Story

As we look to the future, we propose that a contemporary technological metaphor, that software genre, the "adventure game," might be further developed to assist us in moving the ways in which we have come to understand, experience, and interpret collaborative inquiry and design. The metaphor provides some possibilities for evolving pedagogical strategies to support and sustain shared exploration and risk taking. We also have a sense that the adventure game metaphor is one that most students of any age find accessible. Computer-based adventure games provide platforms for exploratory interactions across multilayered narrative frames. These games' relatively open architectures support varied event sequences, action time-spaces, and decision paths. Their hierarchical yet capacious structures support experiential learning—more creative and complex responses are required in the face of surprising and ever more challenging contexts. Multimedia representations heighten sensory and aesthetic engagement. Navigational tools are often incorporated to assist players in mapping their journey, thereby providing connections across time, events, and places. There are even systems of accountability to track resources used and report progress made. Perhaps most important, the concept of *gaming* shapes emotional and intellectual engagement, encouraging playful, often novel responses; whereas the concept of *adventure* anticipates, even welcomes, uncertainty, ambiguity, and challenge.

Of course the multiplayer, real-time, socially interactive version of *Adventures in Education and Democracy* does not exist. Without such a game on the shelf, we attempt to support our students in moving from conventional situational assessments and implementation assumptions to more imaginative and innovative approaches by asking them once more to develop strategic narratives. We present small working groups with a specific implementation challenge that is relevant both to their school design and to their service learning experiences. We ask them to converse and then compose first a short story and later a one-act play.

In the short story challenge, the small groups need to draw directly from their prior experiences in anticipating likely implementation problems and then formulating narrative solution paths. Typically, participants will anticipate familiar blockages and enact response strategies featuring politics and pedagogies that are initially promising but then prove difficult to sustain. After these stories are shared and discussed, the one-act play is assigned. This time, the group members are asked to imagine themselves within the context of an adventure game and to construct a short scenario to be performed in class. For the students, this assignment raises several new challenges. First, their deliberations are complicated by their experiences in developing and analyzing their recent short story narratives. Second, the one-act play assignment requires more advanced conversation and composition skills (and courage for those wary of dramatic performance) in that the groups must consider physical settings, positioning, and movement; tone of voice and facial expressions; scripting the words their characters will speak; and determining the response strategies to be explored. Third, specific constraints of the adventure game are imposed, including conflicting advocacy positions extended from their short stories; intensive accountability pressures; rapidly shifting resource configurations; and new implementation crises. Perhaps most challenging is a central gaming logic that disallows oppositional, nonegalitarian, and deferentially hierarchical approaches to problem solving.

We expect several outcomes here. Adventure game composers and players will encounter new challenges and glimpse new possibilities for analysis and action. They will inevitably experience considerable onset frustration around the demands posed by the developing situations and the novel game logic. Yet they will also find in their previous strategic experiences, some existing and buildable bridges that can be used to reach desired locations in the evolving environment. Our strongest hope is that in drafting the adventure scenarios together our students will discover that they do possess the resources necessary to initiate and to sustain collaborative risk taking.

For us, the adventure game metaphor is helpful in shifting our imaginations from defensive stories of individual heroics in the face of uncaring, seemingly unassailable bureaucratic systems to more proactive tales of communal inquiry, innovation, and change. Using the technologies of transformative listening, *metaphoric thinking,* and daring *social composition,* we can deepen and extend our experience and expression of social courage and resourcefulness.

Further, although we do not need state-of-the-art information technologies to recast collaborative work in education and democratic politics, we can imagine and advocate for advances in hardware and software design and configuration that could enhance and extend our efforts (Kurth-Schai and Green n.d.). We can work together to shape a collaborative transition from current conferencing and simulation software toward systems that encourage more inclusive design premises; support interactive strategic narratives; and integrate deep planning scenarios to facilitate exploratory listening and creative, responsible social action. Over time, our experience as postindustrial, postmodern artists can lead us toward collaborative development of new technologies more supportive of the radically social, ethical, imaginative, aesthetic, and exploratory forms of education necessary for maturing and sustaining democracy.

Two dozen months from now, we can envision the alumni of our course coming back on campus to work with the current students, community members, and a team of software developers on pieces of an information technology. Most of the participants want to ease access to the resources for imagination, make communication as seamless as possible, and lower the technical thresholds for multimedia presentations. Conversations are bounded by what the participants have experienced. Current students are struggling with the demands of the course and are a bit annoyed with this seemingly ambiguous task. Most of the educational community members, still connected to their struggles with conferencing systems, multimedia software packages, and even with their e-mail and word processing, are challenged by this shared design opportunity. The software team is still tentative in its interactions. They are confused by this radically new client relationship but intrigued with many of the items of the wish lists that are emerging. The course alumni seem more comfortable with the ambiguities and risks in this challenge, a bit more facile in spinning "what if" scenarios, and are very attentive listeners in the many conversations under way. It is apparent that significant exchanges are taking place. The classroom is noisy and somewhat disordered. There is an exciting air of uncertainty and unresolved tension about the work. It seems to be a moment for re-envisioning technologies for education and democracy.

Note

1. Nicenet is one technology that provides versatile and dynamic possibilities. It is used widely in kindergarten through twelfth grade and higher education settings. We have deployed it in many different courses over the past three years to post documents and course rosters; to provide conferencing, scheduling and personal messaging; and to note connections to course-relevant Web sites. We have used it not only to extend our classroom time but also to include community members and other consultants in course conversations and project development processes.

References

Apple, Michael. 1993. *Official Knowledge: Democratic Education in a Conservative Age.* New York: Routledge.

Barber, Benjamin. 1984. *Strong Democracy: Participatory Politics for a New Age.* Berkeley: University of California Press.

———. 1992. *The Aristocracy of Everyone: The Politics of Education and the Future of America.* New York: Oxford University Press.

Bickford, Susan. 1996. *The Dissonance of Democracy: Listening, Conflict, and Citizenship.* Ithaca, N.Y.: Cornell University Press.

Bowers, C. A. 1993. *Education, Cultural Myths, and the Ecological Crisis: Toward Deep Changes.* Albany: State University of New York Press.

Bromley, Hank, and Michael Apple, eds. 1998. *Education/Technology/Power: Educational Computing as a Social Practice.* Albany: State University of New York Press.

Burbules, Nicholas. 1997. "Aporia: Webs, Passages, Getting Lost, and Learning to Go On." Pp. 33–43 in *Philosophy of Education 1997.* Urbana, Ill: Philosophy of Education Society.

Burstein, Andrew. 1995. *The Inner Jefferson.* Charlottsville: University of Virginia.

Callister, Thomas. 1994. "Educational Computing's New Direction: Cautiously Approaching an Unpredictable Future." *Educational Theory* 44: 239–256.

Carroll, John. 1997. "Human–Computer Interaction: Psychology as a Science of Design." *Annual Review of Psychology.* Edited by Janet Spence. 48: 61–83.

Cogan, John, and Ray Derricott, eds. 1998. *Citizenship for the Twentieth Century: An International Perspective on Education.* London: Kogan Page.

Connolly, William. 1991. *Identity/Difference: Democratic Negotiations of Political Paradox.* Ithaca: Cornell University Press.

Croft, Richard S. 1993–94. "What Is a Computer in the Classroom? A Deweyan Philosophy for Technology in Education." *Journal of Educational Technology Systems* 22: 301–308.

Dewey, John. 1984. *Democracy and Education.* 1916. Reprint, New York: Macmillan.

Egan, Kieran. 1997. *The Educated Mind: How Cognitive Tools Shape Our Understanding.* Chicago: University of Chicago Press.

Ellis, Joseph J. 1998. *The American Sphinx.* New York: Knopf.

Festenstein, Matthew. 1997. *Pragmatism and Political Theory: From Dewey to Rorty.* Chicago: University of Chicago Press.

Garrison, Jim. 1996. "A Deweyan Theory of Democratic Listening." *Educational Theory* 46: 429–451.

———. 1997. *Dewey and Eros: Wisdom and Desire in the Art of Teaching.* New York: Teachers College Press.

Hickman, Larry N. 1990. *John Dewey's Pragmatic Technology.* Bloomington: Indiana University Press.

Johnson, Mark. 1993. *Moral Imagination: Implications of Cognitive Science for Ethics.* Chicago: University of Chicago Press.

Kahne, Joseph. 1996. *Educational Policy: Democracy, Community and the Individual.* New York: Teachers College Press.

Kane, Jeffrey, ed. 1999. *Education, Information and Transformation: Essays on Learning and Thinking.* Upper Saddle River, N.J.: Merrill–Prentice Hall.

Kurth-Schai, Ruthanne. 1991. "Educational Systems Design by Children for Children." *Educational Foundations* 5: 19–42.

Kurth-Schai, Ruthanne, and Charles R. Green. 1997. "Schooling Stories: Three Paths, Two Tragedies, and One Vision." In *Tales of the State: Narrative in Contemporary U.S. Politics and Public Policy.* Edited by Sanford F. Schram and Philip T. Neissen. New York: Rowman and Littlefield.

———. n.d. "Re-Envisioning Technologies for Education and Democracy." *Progressive Perspectives.* In press.

Lanham, Richard A. 1993. *The Electronic Word: Democracy, Technology, and the Fine Arts.* Chicago: University of Chicago Press.

Lehman, Karl. 1985. *Thomas Jefferson: American Humanist.* Charlottesville: University of Virginia Press.

Linestone, Harold, and Murray Turoff, eds. 1975. *The Delphi Method: Techniques and Applications.* Reading, Mass.: Addison-Wesley.

Lummis, C. Douglas. 1996. *Radical Democracy.* Ithaca: Cornell University Press.

Malone, Dumas. 1948. *Jefferson and His Times.* Boston: Little Brown.

Norman, Donald A. 1992. *Things that Made Us Smart: Defending Human Attributes in the Age of the Machine.* Reading, Mass.: Addison-Wesley.

———. 1998. *The Invisible Computer.* Cambridge: MIT Press.

O'Riley, Patricia. 1996. "A Different Storytelling of Technology Education; Curriculum Revisions: A Storytelling of Difference." *Journal of Technology Education* 7: 28–40.

Palincsar, Sullivan. 1998. "Social Constructivist Perspectives on Teaching and Learning." *Annual Review of Psychology.* Edited by Janet Spence. 49:345–75.

Patrina, Stephan, and Kenneth S. Volk. 1998. "Policy Processes and the Delphi Technique in STS Curricula. *Bulletin of the Science Technology Society* 12: 299–303.

Raboy, Marc, and Peter A. Bruk, eds. 1989. *Communication For and Against Democracy.* Montreal: Blackrose Press.

Sandel, Michael J. 1996. *Democracy's Discontent: America in Search of a Public Philosophy.* Cambridge: Belknap Press of Harvard University Press.

Schacter, Daniel L., Kenneth Norman, and Wilma Koustaal. 1998. "The Cognitive Neuroscience of Constructive Memory." *Annual Review of Psychology.* Edited by Janet Spence. 49: 289–318.a.

Schrage, Michael. 1990. *Shared Minds: The New Technologies of Collaboration.* New York: Random House.

Sclove, Richard. 1995. *Democracy and Technology.* New York and London: Guilford.

Zargari, Ahmad, Charles Partick, and Charles Coddington. 1996. "Objectives of Technology Education: A Philosophical Perspective." *Bulletin of Science Technology Society* 16(4): 178–82.

Correspondence should be addressed to Ruthanne Kurth-Schai, Education Department, Macalester College, 1600 Grand Avenue, St. Paul, MN 55105.

Integrating Computer Technology: Blurring the Roles of Teachers, Students, and Experts

DARA H. WEXLER
Syracuse University

As we approach the twenty-first century, many educators are spending money to wire all classrooms to the Internet. Large amounts of money and energy are being devoted to getting schools "connected." But what does getting connected actually mean to schools? How will schools be changed with the increased integration of computer technology into curricula? The investigation into how technology is being negotiated around issues of power within one specific educational community, the Living SchoolBook,[1] is the focus of this article. Using qualitative research methodologies (participant observations, interviews, and ethnographic techniques), I coded for three themes of power that are centered on the role of the expert found in educational settings. These roles include (1) adults in conventional expert roles, (2) students as experts of technology or content, and (3) students as experts of both technology and content. These themes all contain forms of negotiation, resistance, and regulating practices around the uses of technology in education.

In this article I explore the changing roles of teachers, students, and experts when computer technology is integrated into educational activities. Although I do not claim to hold answers regarding this integration, I do identify some of these changing roles and raise questions for further study.

Built into the use of technology is a power dynamic that includes the tension between acceptance and denial of how to use technology and who will use the technology. Typically, adults are in the position of power within schools and are deemed educators, whereas youth are subjugated as learners. How learners and educators understand and deal with the use of technology and how this technology is introduced into various learning environments constructs a tension between those who know and those who do not know how to use technology. These tensions of knowledge are continuously being negotiated, many times with shifts occurring in pedagogy and practice.

This investigation focuses on three issues pertaining to the Living SchoolBook: (1) What makes this a unique technological learning community; (2) what are the shifting roles of learners and educators; and (3) what are the struggles of negotiating my roles as consultant, editor, and researcher within this particular community?

A Unique Technological Learning Environment:
The Living SchoolBook

> The Living SchoolBook (LSB) is a collaborative, electronic learning community. Founded on the belief that new technology can facilitate and inspire the best work of teachers and students, the LSB encourages and enables the collaboration of educators, students, and professionals in the development and implementation of technology-based projects....Teachers and students from K–12 schools and universities have designed and created on-line projects that demonstrate student inquiry, problem-solving, and collaboration. (Living SchoolBook Staff 2000, online citation)

Although there are many ways to integrate technology into educational spaces, what makes LSB a unique community is that it is made up of both physical and virtual educational spaces. Physical educational spaces include the actual middle and high schools, a university school of education, the LSB lab, and the project director's office. These places can be considered traditional types of spaces. Virtual educational spaces are created by the computer-networked communications between the physical spaces and the communities of educators that are formed through these collaborations. Howard Rheingold described virtual communities as a place to exchange ideas with others without being there in body:

> People in virtual communities use words on screens to exchange pleasantries and argue, engage in intellectual discourse, conduct commerce, exchange knowledge, share emotional support, make plans, brainstorm, gossip, feud, fall in love, find friends and lose them, play games, flirt, create a little high art and a lot if idle talk. People in virtual communities do just about everything people do in real life, but we leave our bodies behind. You can't kiss anybody and nobody can punch you in the nose, but a lot can happen within those boundaries. (Rheingold 1998, online citation)

Although this idea of a virtual community is similar to the LSB community in that it provides a space to communicate, it differs in that people are connected to their bodies; people meet face-to-face as well as virtually in order to plan, exchange thoughts, collaborate, and build educational projects. Also, whereas Rheingold referred to using "words on screens," the LSB goes beyond this notion of a virtual community by also utilizing videoconferencing capabilities that allow for visual and auditory exchanges.

The LSB community is made up of a unique combination of teacher teams, researchers, and community agencies and media, telecommunications, and hardware specialists who collaboratively create interactive learning environments both inside and outside of the classroom. Projects are generated by utilizing multiple forms of media and tools such as digital cameras, scanners, videoconferencing, TVs and VCRs, web design, lab cams, dialoguing capabilities, software, and digital video that all contribute to the development of interdisciplinary projects and collaborations. The LSB takes a collaborative approach in the ways it operates on a day-to-day basis as well as how projects are proposed and developed by teachers, students, staff members, and outside agencies. Projects are cross-disciplinary; involve using the Internet as a work space, a final product, or both; and draw on utilizing a variety of media forms.

The LSB began six years ago as a research-and-development project consisting of a wide-bandwidth computer network connecting three schools in upstate New York through New York State funding. The initial goal of the project was to see what would happen when cutting-edge technologies were put directly into the hands of educators. Whereas initially, these educators consisted of kindergarten through twelfth grade (K–12) teachers, over the past five years, the term *educators* has grown to encompass both K–12 and higher education students and faculty as well as community agencies and technology partners.

Three K–12 schools located in upstate New York—two high schools and one middle school—are directly wired by high-speed connections to the LSB, which resides in the School of Education at Syracuse University. These connections allow for file sharing and problem solving at a distance, videoconferencing capabilities, professional development, access to university and K–12 resources, and on-demand support for project development. Each of these K–12 schools has between three and eight teachers who have volunteered to work with the LSB over the past five years. These teachers have a wide range of technological abilities and each of their schools have very different computer setups and school cultures.

Shifting Roles of Learners and Educators

Technology is entangled within a power/knowledge structure where the ability to use technology, and the knowledge related to technology, are often privileged. Through this power/knowledge dynamic, technology becomes a space where authority and expertise play a key role. According to Foucault, "What makes power hold good, what makes it accepted, is simply the fact that it doesn't only weigh on us as a force that says no, but that it traverses and produces things, it induces pleasure, forms knowledge, produces discourse. It needs to be considered as a productive network, which runs through the whole social body, much more than as a negative instance whose function is repressive" (Foucault 1980, 119).

Drawing on Foucault's description of power as being a productive force enables educators to frame technology as a curricular issue, one that is central to how education is changing (or should be changing?) to compensate for these shifts in power/knowledge. The relations and tensions that exist between education and technology have created an ambiguous space of power where these two domains cannot exist independent of one another.

Within LSB projects, those who are defined as the learners and the educators have become blurred. Although students (i.e., young people) are typically the learners, and teachers (i.e., adults) are typically the educators, the nature of working on collaborative technology projects tends to shift the traditional authoritative power dynamics of the teacher passing knowledge down to the student. In addition, LSB collaborative technology project-based educational activities help to further break down the boundaries between K–12 and higher education students, teachers, and researchers because the LSB community interacts with all of these groups as well as allows for contributors to shift roles throughout a project or between projects. Therefore, the shifting of who is a learner and who is an educator is constantly being blurred, depending on the learning activities taking place. Although this blurring of boundaries between learner and educator are in constant flux, teachers and students are struggling with negotiating these shifts in power.

Expanding the Role of the Expert

Experts in a K–12 setting traditionally tend to be adults who are physically brought into the classroom as guest speakers, or students are brought to an expert through a field trip experience. The LSB has assisted with bringing experts to the schools in both traditional senses (i.e., guest speakers and field trips) as well as by connecting experts and resources to schools through technology in more nontraditional ways. Following are three examples of shifts in the power/knowledge of an expert: (1) conventional expert roles within a technological environment, (2) students as experts of technology or content, and (3) students as experts of technology and content.

Conventional Expert Roles Within a Technological Environment

One example of a conventional expert role occurred when two art professors at Syracuse University's Visual and Performing Arts program videoconferenced with advanced drawing, painting, and multimedia classes at one of the high schools associated with LSB. These students and professors were able to show their artwork to one another even though they were at a distance. The professors critiqued the students' work and the students had the opportunity to ask about careers in art-related fields and what to include in their portfolios when applying for jobs or graduate programs.

A second example involved high-school social studies students at another LSB-associated high school who videoconferenced with the associate director of Syracuse University's Art Museum on Works Progress Administration (WPA) art. This professor reviewed the students' analytical essays about WPA art and offered them feedback. When the students came to Syracuse University to present their research to a group of LSB teachers, they met the professor in person and were given a tour of the art archives. Regarding this project, Mr. Crocker, the social studies teacher, said,

> As far as the future goes, one of the things that I would like to see more of is more collaborating between our site and the kids that are part of that and the other kids in other places around the state and the country. That needs to be done. I think one of the great things about this whole project is that it helps conquer the distance.

By connecting kids with other kids around the state, the more conventional expert roles begin to break down as students themselves become experts to other kids.

Students as Experts

Although many higher education professors and K–12 teachers may possess content knowledge, they do not always possess technology knowledge. With so many schools purchasing computers and requiring students to become computer literate, many teachers are realizing that they do not have the necessary skills to teach in the same manner as they have in the past. Therefore, in a technological space such as the LSB, I have seen the label "expert" stretch to also cover students at both the K–12 and higher education levels. The roles of learners and educators are blurring and people are taking on multiple roles simultaneously. One way to see this shift of the student as expert is around educational content.

Students as Experts of Content

Pre-service science student teachers at Syracuse University assisted the LSB with a collaborative CD-ROM project about Onondaga Lake, described as a "tour of natural habitats [that] has been created to help dispel the perception of Onondaga Lake as a desolate, polluted area. Emphasis is on the surrounding ecosystem of the lake, rather than on the waters. Areas included are adjacent wetlands, meadows, woodland, as well as brush areas describing wildlife and plants."[2]

University pre-service science students functioned as content experts on environmental habitats and animals while working at a distance with middle-school students who were part of an after-school program. These pre-service students were in the ambiguous space of being expert educators as well as being learners (i.e., learning to become teachers while still struggling with the negotiation of educational pedagogy and practice). Although they were seen as novices on one hand, they were seen as experts on another.

Students as Experts of Technology

The same ambiguity of being experts can be applied to K–12 students whose knowledge is typically not valued in schools. But in a technology environment, the traditional norms of power and knowledge—who has authority and who does not—become blurred. Students who have knowledge that their teachers lack often become valued, although this is still dependent upon the teachers' control and whether or not they are willing to let the students explore their ideas. Teachers who acknowledge their students' knowledge begin to understand the value of integrating technology into learning. As one teacher said, "I have kids that might be interested in going way beyond what I know in terms of using our machinery here." On another occasion he said, "I am not the high peak of information that I thought I was. My credibility is shot there."

These are the types of comments made by teachers who are beginning to see the possibilities of shifting authority and are willing to let go of some of their power in the classroom. As Ms. Chase, a high-school English and journalism teacher, said,

> The kids lead me on computers.… Now we're on a Mac and we do Aldus Pagemaker. I say we, they do. I sit. I watch. I get excited. I try to facilitate. I try to run interference if they need funding for this or that but that's my only experience prior to this. I knew nothing about the Internet. I knew nothing about videoconferencing. I still would consider myself someone who's an initiate, not an expert by any means. But it just seems so exciting to think that there could be so many new ways of gathering information and making my classroom a more lively place.

With university students working directly with K–12 students on specific projects of interest (e.g., developing web pages for classroom projects), the traditional teacher role is erased from the learning process and a new teacher role emerges.

Students as Experts of Content and Technology

The greatest shift in power and valued knowledge seems to reconstruct and reshape the teacher role, as described by Pedro, who emerged as a student expert of both content and technology. Pedro was a high-school student the LSB was working with who had recently emigrated from Mexico, spoke English as a second language, and had a great interest in working with technology. Pedro began playing around with computers and technology in his school and then began helping both teachers and students. As Mrs. Cathcart, the staff developer who worked closely with him, wrote,

> Pedro is a young man who has a gift for understanding technology. Living in a very poor urban community, cultivating this talent might be an

opportunity for Pedro to develop a lucrative future. His multifaceted involvement with LSB projects is allowing him an opportunity of a lifetime. He has learned immeasurably from being on these machines almost daily. His self-esteem and confidence have improved, his speaking is much more understandable and confident. He has learned skills that will be helpful. He now has a part-time job in a computer store after school and still serves as a student and staff mentor, technician, and troubleshooter.

But Pedro not only had an interest and talent in working with technology, he also served as an expert of content. He began videoconferencing with Spanish level-one middle-school students. As described by Mrs. Barnes, the Spanish teacher,

> Our teleconferencing experience has been wonderful this year. My seventh period class meets with a student (recently emigrated from Mexico) now attending [name of high school], every other Tuesday or Wednesday. The students take turns talking in Spanish on such topics as school, family, weather, pastime activities, and favorite things. We usually name a topic a few days before the teleconference and include some possible questions, and the students take it from there.

Because Pedro is a native Spanish-speaking student, he was able to provide a resource unavailable to a majority of introductory Spanish classes—a young person who has an authentic Spanish pronunciation and accent. As Mrs. Cathcart said,

> The kids were hesitant and timid at first, as was Pedro, a young man who had only a few months of being in the United States under his belt. As our biweekly sessions progressed, the kids began to recognize each other and they were more apt to risk answering without first looking to the teacher for help. Pedro's authentic accent was a challenge, but through time, kids appeared to understand him more easily.

Collaborative mentors working with other students and teachers can provide certain areas of expertise that traditional teachers may not be able to provide. With the integration of technology into education, experts can be students, teachers, or both in either K–12 or higher education.

Role Confusion: Consultant, Editor, or Researcher?

Just as the previous paragraphs demonstrated the shifting of boundaries around who is a learner, an educator, and an expert, I find my roles shifting as well. I am constantly negotiating these roles on a daily basis through my interactions with teachers, students, and community agencies. I have been a graduate research assistant with the LSB for the past five years. Over this course of time I have had the opportunity to develop working relationships with the many teachers, students, and collaborative partners, learning about various technologies, and I have been invited into teachers' classrooms as both a researcher and consultant.

Part of my job has been to gather the natural history of the project, participate in presentations and demonstrations of the LSB for various audiences (e.g., university classes, conference presentations, and demonstrations for political figures) as well as function as one of two field coordinators for teacher–student projects on a day-to-day basis. Reflecting on these activities has enabled me to see the potential and the drawbacks of technology integration into education. But, although the more obvious pluses and minuses stand out around issues of access and software constraints, issues of power are implicitly embedded within the dynamics of who uses technology and who does not as well as in what ways at what points in time. These power relationships are typical of educational spaces but are especially poignant at this historical moment when technology is being seen as essential to educational curricula.

The struggle I am constantly involved in revolves around the questions Who am I? and How am I being seen? Negotiating the roles of (1) being a consultant for the integration of technology into curricula for teachers and students, (2) being a Web site editor for student and teacher work, or (3) being an educational researcher and knowing how to make meaning from new media texts (such as Web sites, e-mail, and videoconferencing communications) is especially difficult when these roles cannot always be separate from one another. In addition, these roles have power relationships built into them and are always shifting in importance. Although I do not claim to have answers regarding the struggles embedded within my roles, I do provide some questions to think about.

Collecting Content and Working on a Day-to-Day Basis

- At what point in the project construction process should I edit student and teacher work?
- Can editing this work change the content or learning process?

Usually when a student hands in a paper for a grade, it is between the student and the teacher (and on occasion, a parent or another student), but now the power of the Internet enables work to be seen by the student, the teacher, and possibly anyone in the world. The powerful nature of technology lends itself to sharing student work with a wider audience than the typical schoolwork audience and therefore creates an increased concern for the LSB field coordinators (including myself) pertaining to editing student work that will be appearing on the Web.

When working with the New York State Historical Art project,[3] students would e-mail or send me descriptions, drawings, and photographs of what they wanted me to put up on the Web site for them. They described in words how they would like their Web site laid out and where they would like the text to be placed. I would then go in and make these changes in HTML (the language that is used to create Web pages). But when I found spelling or grammar errors, I was not sure if I should be the one to make these editorial changes. The same issue arose with the CyberZoo[4] project when the English and science teachers wanted me to change student mistakes a year after the assignment had been due. Where do you draw the line when a project is finished? Is a project ever finished? Does making these editorial changes influence the content on a Web page or the student learning processes? How about the teacher's learning processes?

Knowing When to Research and When Not To

- Do my research questions change the learner's or educator's learning process or decisions because I may be seen as having an expertise that they feel they do not have?
- Do my research questions change the learner's or educator's decisions about technology usage since I may be seen as having an expertise that they feel they do not have?

Being unsure of when to be a researcher and when not to be is an ongoing dilemma for me. Knowing when to simply observe and record teachers and students and when to offer suggestions and advice creates a conflict between being a researcher and being a consultant, but oddly, both are part of my job. One example of this conflict occurred during the summer of 1998 at a LSB Teacher Institute meeting. I was unsure when, and how often, I shifted from being a consultant to a researcher during a meeting when two English teachers, one library media specialist, and I were talking about, and planning for, a course the two teachers would be teaching in September. They asked questions pertaining to using various forms of technology, but I was never sure how long I should let them struggle with their questions before I stepped in and offered my guidance.

I was also unsure about when and if it would be okay for me to tape-record our discussion. I did not want to disrupt the conversation flow or position myself as a researcher or a consultant, but at the same time I did not want to lose rich data. Although I did not think that they would mind being tape-recorded, as they have been part of this research project for over four years, I still struggled over the decision of whether or not to ask them. I did not want them to stop asking me for advice, and I did not want to disrupt their brainstorming session. How does my role (however they choose to see me) influence their decisions about trying new technologies when they often see me as having an expertise that they feel they do not have?

Conclusion

The blurring of teacher, student, and expert roles can happen when schools connect to the Internet. When these roles blur, negotiations around the issues of power and knowledge in schools occur.

In this article I attempted to explore these changing roles and provide some questions pertaining to the integration of computer technology into educational curricula. In addition, exploring the tensions that emerge between the shifting roles of learners and educators, as well as understanding my struggles in negotiating the roles of consultant, editor, and researcher, represent crucial issues in the use of technology and content knowledge. Although the LSB is just one unique community, the lessons learned from this community can most likely be applied to other emerging educational communities integrating technology into their schools.

Questions remain about how to study new media texts such as Web sites, videoconferences, and e-mail that are used for project-based learning communities like the LSB. What kinds of methodological questions need to be addressed when working with, and studying about, these new media texts? And what kinds of qualitative methods would be helpful in researching? As I begin to explore these new territories that involve the integration of technology into education, I can see roles changing both within and outside of schools.

Notes

1. The Living SchoolBook (LSB), now in its sixth year of operation, is a research and development project that works to integrate new technology into educational curricula. Because the LSB has been publicized in newspapers, reports, and in schools, its name has not been changed, although specific teacher and student names have been changed.
2. To learn more about the Onondaga Lake Wildlife Habitat Awareness project, visit the Living SchoolBook Web site: http://lsb.syr.edu/projects/onondagalake/Onondaga Lake New
3. To learn more about the History Through New York State Art and the New Deal Art projects, visit the Living SchoolBook Web site: http://lsb.syr.edu/projects/newdeal/
4. To learn more about the CyberZoo project, visit the Living SchoolBook Web site: http://lsb.syr.edu/projects/cyberzoo/

References

Foucault, Michel. 1980. "Truth and Power." Pp. 109–133 in *Power/Knowledge: Selected Interviews & Other Writings 1972–1977*. Edited by Colin Gordon and translated by Colin Gordon, Leo Marshall, John Mepham, and Kate Soper. New York: Pantheon.

Living SchoolBook Staff. 2000. Living SchoolBook Web site http://lsb.syr.edu Accessed 5 February 2000.

Rheingold, Howard. 1998. *The Virtual Community: Homesteading on the Electronic Frontier* [book online]. Reading, Mass.: Addison-Wesley, 1993. Available from the Howard Rheingold Web site: http://www.rheingold.com/vc/book/intro.html Accessed 28 December 1998.

Correspondence should be addressed to Dara H. Wexler, Cultural Foundations of Education, Syracuse University, 350 Huntington Hall, Syracuse, NY 13244.

BOOK REVIEWS

Collective Intelligence: Mankind's Emerging World in Cyberspace. Pierre Levy (translated from the French by Robert Bononno). New York: Plenum Trade, 1997. pp. xxviii, 277.

LINA LOPEZ CHIAPPONE
University of Miami

The proliferation of computers and the emergence of digital technologies have led us to a dynamic period in our social history. Communication occurs at lightning speed, information is easily disseminated, and movement is redefined as technology bridges the space between people and ideas. Along with creating a global community, we are in the process of defining ourselves in an evolving cyberculture. Pierre Levy, professor of hypermedia at the University of Paris, provides a vision for this emerging network of ideas in his book *Collective Intelligence: Mankind's Emerging World in Cyberspace.*

Levy's thesis is straightforward. He is convinced that cyberspace has the potential to have immense repercussions for our economic, political, and cultural lives. According to him, cyberspace is a "mode of creation and navigation within knowledge" (10). Contemporary humankind's new frontier is the knowledge space, and we are in the unique position to develop and use information technology not to replace humanity but to "promote intelligent communities in which our social and cognitive potential can be mutually developed and enhanced" (10).

Levy draws from the fields of anthropology, history, economics, sociology, and philosophy, weaving themes from these disciplines in his analysis of the communication revolution. He explains how we are ushering in a new model of humanity and culture in a computer-based society, much like the earlier transition from oral culture in the medieval period to the print-based culture of the Renaissance. Further, he argues that unlike our ancestors whose lives were driven by emerging technologies, we are in a unique position to define how new technologies are used, who controls them, and what their ultimate goals will be. His arguments, though abstract and diverse, explore the often-ignored human component of technology and forge a series of new ideas, which, although somewhat romantic and utopian, inspire the charting of a new course as we navigate the ever-widening complexity known as cyberspace.

Levy views cyberspace as a commune of the mind, where information is shared and everyone reaps the benefits of this feast or cornucopia of ideas. He explains how the idea of a collective intelligence was first described between the tenth and twelfth centuries by Persian and Jewish mystics. In their work, they described the idea of a collective consciousness that focused on an active *agent intellect*—one that constantly contemplates true ideas and that enables human intelligences to become active (92). According to mystics like Al-Farabi and Ibn Sina, receptive souls receive illumination from the agent intellect, and potential intelligence in humans becomes an active intelligence. All humanity shares the agent intellect and is linked to a knowing divinity rather than an all-powerful God. Levy is also influenced by French philosophical thought and socialist egalitarian ideas that logically follow from these ancient notions of self-reflective thinking. "The agent intellect becomes the expression, the space of communication, navigation, and negotiation among the members of a collective intellect" (97). To Levy, entering the collective intelligence becomes almost a divine act in which the contributors become responsible for nurturing this dynamic body of knowledge. This astute comparison of today's virtual worlds and cyberspace with centuries-old ideas emphasizes his premise that although mankind is at the threshold of something new, the fundamental principles at work are inherent to humanity and have arisen out of a human need to self-improve, grow, and belong.

Levy addresses how knowledge and its management confer power. Communities exhibiting imagination, initiative, and rapid response will ensure their success in the rapidly developing information arenas. Networks of knowledge must be flexible and dynamic; ideas must be allowed to flow, interact, and change. "Once the process of renewal slows down, the company or organization is in danger of petrification and extinction" (2). Additionally, the individual must continuously renew his or her intellectual potential, and successful organizations are those in which the individual is involved in its planning. Knowledge becomes the new infrastructure. As information contributors and seekers, Levy argues we are burdened with perpetuating the collective space where a new type of intelligence is formed. One cannot enter this space without changing it and having it change the participant. In doing so, this question arises: With God no longer as the knowledge giver, have we replaced God with cyberspace? Levy's arguments seem to confuse our role in the collective space with true divinity.

Levy crystallizes his cyberspace philosophy by using the metaphor of a nomad to explain how "nomadism of today reflects the continuous and rapid transformation of scientific, technical, economic, professional, and mental landscapes" (xxiii). Civilization's new horizon is the knowledge space in which the process of renewal and innovation occur in the new cultural geography of cyberspace. In this context, new systems like the Internet become a vast meeting place of minds that will not be subjected to free-market ideas and capitalism. Levy explains how the exchange of ideas has a liberating effect for the individual, who is valued for con-

tributing to the collective intelligence. Humanity must develop new ways of thinking and adding to the collective intelligence if progress is to be made and the
knowledge space is to be fully explored. "The major architectural project of the
twenty-first century will be to imagine, build, and enhance an interactive and
ever-changing cyberspace" (10).

Levy humanizes the task of building the architecture for the new millennium
by underscoring "a new bearing, a new vision, a kind of utopia: renewal of the
social bond through our relation to knowledge" (11). In Part 1 of the book, he
deftly argues that current forms of social bonds based on ethnicity, nationality,
and religion, for example, are collapsing because there is no perceived frame of
reference or sense of identity and therefore has led to confrontations worldwide.
By establishing social bonds based on our relationship to knowledge,
"deterritorialized civility" (11) is developed; we interact, exchange information,
and bring knowledge to life. By deterritorializing in this manner, we begin to
identify ourselves as knowledge entities. A stranger is not seen as threatening
but as someone who has knowledge that I do not have. There is then an immediate exchange, and each person is valued for contributing that knowledge. The
value of the individual takes center stage. "Even though I am unemployed, or
without money or a diploma, condemned to life in a ghetto, illiterate, I am not
useless. I am not interchangeable. I have an image, a position, dignity, a personal and positive value within the knowledge space" (13).

Deterritorialization forms the basis for Levy's premise of a collective intelligence, a form of universally distributed intelligence. The strength of Levy's book
is the convincing argument that knowledge is the sum of what we know and we all
play an important role in developing it. Levy attacks the "organization of ignorance" (14) in our world, which succeeds in stunting growth, experience, and skill
rather than constantly enhancing it. He believes efficient methods of communication will help members of a community coordinate interactions in cyberspace and
promote the unencumbered exchange of ideas.

Finally, toward the end of the book, Levy returns to the idea of the humanizing
effect of technology. According to him, a new humanism emerges as collective
thought that leads to a sense of community. Levy explains, "Far from merging individual intelligence into some indistinguishable magma, collective intelligence is
a process of growth, differentiation, and tʰ mutual revival of singularities" (15).
Levy continues his metaphor of the nomads and their wanderings in Part 2 of the
book, which includes further discussion of the knowledge space and its continued
state of "emerging." The metaphor that emphasized "wandering" evolves into one
of a voyager following guidance devices and other tools to reach a destination. The
juxtaposition of metaphors symbolizes for us the hope that we have progressed beyond mere wanderings and whims and are approaching the utopia of collective intelligence that, although still a "free" space, can be navigated with ease. The
voyages in these virtual worlds will be of "self-knowledge and self-definition for

humanity, which can then form itself into autonomous and autopoietic (self-renewing) collective intellects" (98).

Levy's mystical ideas about cyberspace are a far departure from those of some Americans who see it primarily as a business opportunity and not as a commonly shared space for dialogue and interaction. He forges a philosophy that will guide humanity in using this new tool as it works to renew and redefine itself. In his epilogue, Levy explains how in this process of renewal, a new and more true type of democracy emerges, one in which individuals actively participate in shaping the culture and society. Levy's prophetic vision can be seen in today's headlines with the grass-roots campaign via the Internet of Governor Ventura in Minnesota. Perhaps the sharing of knowledge in virtual worlds can redemocratize our complacent democracy with a self-renewing collective intelligence. Virtual worlds have the potential to reflect the intellectual light that comes from humanity, which in turn will continue to grow and prosper. These ideas of self-determination and the movement away from totalitarian control are reminiscent of the 1960s romantic radicalism; however, Levy revisits them in the context of this new phase of evolution and the far-reaching potential of the virtual worlds we are creating.

Levy's book provides an underlying philosophy for the computerization of society, a kind of mission statement for the emergence of cyberspace, replete with lofty goals and carefully outlined tenets. He does not fully address the commercialization of cyberspace, but that alone does not detract from his visionary text. Although some have called this book a blueprint for the cyber era, that would be in direct contradiction to Levy's firmly held belief in a self-determining intellect free of totalitarian control. Whereas a blueprint delineates and demarcates a plan, Levy's mission statement for this new era, while acknowledging the importance of cyberspatial tools such as hypertext and the Internet, also emphasizes the broader humanizing elements of technologies that enable us to think collectively rather than just "haul masses of information around with us" (10). The social bond, shared discourse, and collective intellect define the knowledge space, or cosmopedia, now emerging. Levy's book is a guide with a conscience in this process of "becoming." He sets forth a moral challenge as we explore the vast labyrinth of cyberspace secure in the knowledge that working collectively "humanity has a chance to reclaim its future and shape itself into intelligent communities, capable of negotiating the stormy seas of change" (xxv).

Brave New Schools: Challenging Cultural Illiteracy Through Global Learning Networks. Jim Cummins and Dennis Sayers. New York: St. Martin's Press, 1995. pp. x, 374.

KEITH GRAZIADEI
University of Miami

Jim Cummins and Dennis Sayers close their book *Brave New Schools: Challenging Cultural Illiteracy Through Global Learning Networks* with a comment and question:

> Clearly issues of culture, education and technology merge at the crossroad of the twenty first century. Do we plan for the common good by enabling all students to navigate difference, develop intellectually and academically and gain expertise in employing technology for enhancing democratic participation or do we curtail the development of these social, intellectual and technological skills in order to restrict potential changes to the current distribution of power and resources in our society. (176)

This question is fundamental to those interested in the social foundations of education. Asked in a slightly different form, the question could be: What path do we take in using technology in addressing questions of diversity and equity in our educational system and society as a whole?

Clearly technology, and especially educational computing, is a double-edged sword: "The same technology that opens the world to our consciousness frequently closes our consciousness to the world" (4). Referring in their title to Aldous Huxley's dysutopia, *Brave New World* (1932), Cummins and Sayers in *Brave New Schools* raise issues about the moral dilemmas that confront educators and the public at large through the widespread use of computers in the schools.

Cummins and Sayers believe that through the use of collaborative inquiry, a revolution is possible in education. Although such models have existed in the past, for example, Celestin Freinet's Modern School Movement, which had children collaboratively learn through the exchange of "cultural packages" between schools geographically set apart from one another, the technology to implement this process was limited compared to the power provided by contemporary computer networks like the Internet.

Drawing upon critical theorists such as Paulo Freire and Henry Giroux, Cummins and Sayer begin to establish a model of collaborative critical inquiry that provides a foundation for global learning networks that have the potential to transform contemporary education through the use of technology. Specifically, they address issues such as empowerment, critical literacy, social activism, and relations of power. In this context, they are exploring concepts fundamental to the field of the social foundations of education.

Cummins and Sayers, like Seymour Papert in *The Children's Machine* (1993), believe that the computer—particularly in the form of the Internet—has the potential to act as a liberating technology for the learner. In particular, they maintain that the potential of the computer and the Internet to create collaborative communities contradicts current systems of control that are at work in most contemporary educational settings.

In utilizing global learning networks, the authors employ ideas such as intercultural learning, distancing, reflective teaching, and meaningful literacy production. The authors state their belief that global learning networks serve to act as a catalyst for collaborative critical inquiry. In particular, meaningful literacy production provides a powerful means of developing an intrinsic motivation to learn via the use of global learning networks.

Cummins and Sayers argue that by necessity, a restructuring of schools must consist of increasing achievement for marginalized groups, a redistribution of resources among schools, and most important, a redefining of the mission of schools to include the perspective of diversity as a resource (169). The authors believe that if we are to go beyond a transmission model of education, these components are crucial in developing a critical, as opposed to a functional, literacy.

Brave New Schools: Challenging Cultural Illiteracy Through Global Learning Networks is divided into two main parts. The first lays out the context and aims for combating cultural illiteracy. The second provides an extensive listing of listservs, usenet groups, gopher and Web sites, and other Internet resources that serve as examples for teachers and parents.

The first part of chapter 1 sets the context for the discussion on collaborative critical inquiry in global learning networks. The authors discuss the rise in the use of critical inquiry by educators and the importance this has for the current educational reform debate. The notions of functional literacy versus critical literacy are discussed in this context. *Cultural illiteracy* is defined by Cummins and Sayers as the cultural literacy movement that contains a common core knowledge or canonized Western knowledge currently touted by proponents such as Hirsch (1987) and Ravitch and Finn (1987). The authors also develop the idea of intercultural learning networks and how current technology (e.g., the Internet) can increase the possibilities for different types of learning. At the core of this notion is the idea that educational technology is simply a means, not an end. As the authors explain, it is a "cultural amplifier" used by teachers "to 'turn up the volume' for their faraway colleagues" (15).

Cummins and Sayers begin chapter 2 by posing the question, "Why speak of technology, let alone computer technology, when textbooks…are in such short supply…." (17). Global collaborative exchanges are not necessarily dependent on having access to computer technologies. As Freinet and Lodi demonstrated in the past, meaningful exchanges can be undertaken with minimal technology. But the authors are quick to note that "while access to sophisticated technology is not essential for engaging in intercultural learning networks ... equity of access is a central issue for any serious attempt at educational reform in today's schools" (18). With this as a reference, chapter 2 highlights eight recent projects that involve global learning networks. The two most prominent networks featured and discussed in this section are *I*EARN* and *Orillas*. In particular, the *I*EARN* Veli Joze Refugee Camp Project in Croatia and the *Orillas International Proverbs Project* stand out as two exceptional examples of using collaborative critical inquiry in computerized global learning networks.

Chapter 3 focuses on a discussion of the current educational reform dilemma. The authors discuss current debates between functional literacy (which focuses on skills), cultural literacy (which focuses on content), and critical literacy (which centers on issues of power). The dilemma deals with the cultural, economic, and scientific realities that currently exist in our society and their relations to achieving critical literacy for all. According to Cummins and Sayers, the current power structure is ambivalent to critical literacy, and herein lies the dilemma. How do we achieve cultural literacy when discourses concerning such topics are related to patterns of power relations (92)? The authors' claim that what is needed is a long-term investment in the education of marginalized groups and a model for schools that is based on collaboration and critical thinking (113).

Framed within the current educational reform debate, chapter 4 moves into a historical analysis of global learning networks. Beginning with the work of the previously mentioned French educator Celestin Freinet and the Modern School Movement in 1924, global learning networks are examined as they relate to promoting reflective teaching, student–teacher interactive relationships, and acquisition of literacy through interschool networks. Cummins and Sayers assert that Freinet argued for coherent educational theory based on reflective classroom practices while discarding the fixed rigidity of the curriculum (128). Of significant importance is the discussion of Freinet's literacy process, which involved students writing about familiarities and sharing their work with distant colleagues.

The discussion then moves into the work of Italian educator Mario Lodi and the Italian Cooperative Education Movement during the 1950s. Lodi's comparison of dialects and their use as a platform to build fluency in the language of the wider society is extremely relevant given the contemporary rise in linguistic diversity that exists in American schools (133). Cummins and Sayers conclude this historical overview with the notion that "access to literacy means access to power" (138). They discuss the concept of "gatekeeping" that allows some access to literacy and bars others from it. Ultimately, the success of Freinet's learning network is a result of the "integration of technology with a pedagogy of collaborative critical inquiry" (139).

Chapter 5 deals with placing collaborative critical inquiry within the context of current schooling approaches. Cummins and Sayers discuss traditional, progressive, and transformative models of pedagogy from the perspective of instructional and social assumptions that each of these approaches makes. What results is their claim that "transformative pedagogy uses collaborative critical inquiry to relate curriculum content to students' individual and collective experience and to analyze broader social issues relevant to their lives" (153). Cummins and Sayers further assert that transformative pedagogy is crucial in utilizing global learning networks to their maximum efficiency (153).

The authors also examine Henry Giroux's notion of border crossing in this chapter and agree that schools must create conditions for students to become border crossers and that intercultural learning keeps students open to cultural exchanges (161). They conclude by emphasizing the potential advantages our society will have if we include all "social groups in this process of cultural exchange and ensuring equality of access to these forms of learning"(163).

The final chapter in the book is entitled "Superhighway to Where?" Cummins and Sayers focus on the question of how to navigate difference. They maintain that we have reached a point of diminishing returns in the existing power structure and educational framework (167). Coercive relations of power are no longer adequate or equitable, and we should move toward a more collaborative relation of power. Our society needs to learn "how to work together across cultural and linguistic differences in ways that generate empowerment for all participants" (167). Cummins and Sayers assert that this reform can be achieved if we utilize collaborative critical inquiry in the context of global learning networks (170).

Brave New Schools: Challenging Cultural Illiteracy Through Global Learning Networks has profound implications for those concerned with the role that technology and learning networks play in addressing issues of equity and diversity in our schools and the larger society. Using global learning networks through collaborative critical inquiry is a powerful means of beginning to address issues of power relations and resource distribution within the context of schooling. Raising the awareness of students to these issues goes a long way in establishing a critical literacy movement in education.

Cummins and Sayers force us, as educators, to address how we view technology in our classrooms and in our daily lives and in turn how we can use technology to help achieve a critical literacy. Without asking the essential questions of "Why?" and "For what purpose?" do we use technology, we only serve to blind "our consciousness to the world" (4). According to Cummins and Sayers, "Learning how to control, rather than being controlled by the technology, is essential to education in the twenty-first century" (174). Doing so is not only essential to education, but also, more specifically, to developing a critical literacy within the culture as a whole.

References

Hirsch, E. D. 1987. *Cultural Literacy: What Every American Needs to Know*. Boston: Houghton Mifflin.

Huxley, A. 1932. *Brave New World*. New York: HarperPerennial.

Papert, S. 1993. *The Children's Machine: Rethinking School in the Age of the Computer*. New York: Basic Books.

Ravitch, D., and C. Finn. 1987. *What Do Our 17-Year-Olds Know? A Report on the First National Assessment of History and Literature*. New York: Harper & Row.

Life on the Screen: Identity in the Age of the Internet.

Sherry Turkle. New York: Simon & Schuster, 1995. pp. 347.

LINA LOPEZ CHIAPPONE
University of Miami

With cyberspace and the Internet now becoming humankind's new frontier, we are at a defining moment in contemporary culture. The computer has evolved from a tool used primarily for calculations into the basis for a new culture of simulation and online exploration. In *Life on the Screen: Identity in the Age of the Internet*, Sherry Turkle describes how we are constructing our identities using the Internet and in turn redefining the notion of self. Turkle's book explores how the emerging culture of simulation is affecting our ideas about mind, body, self, and machine. The computer, no longer just a tool, has become a reflection of ourselves, and in the larger cultural context, it is "eroding boundaries between the real and the virtual, the animate and the inanimate, the unitary and the multiple self" (10). This thesis is developed through case studies of computer users that Turkle found compelling and meaningful in explaining the evolving relation between computers and people.

Turkle, a clinical psychologist and professor of the sociology of science at the Massachusetts Institute of Technology, bases this very personal book on roughly one thousand ethnographic and clinical observations of people involved in computer culture. In her earlier seminal book, *The Second Self* (1984), Turkle described the identity-transforming relations people had with computers—relations that were essentially one-on-one, the person alone with a machine, the computer as a mirror of the self. In *Life on the Screen*, Turkle turns to the computer as a collective experience by focusing her attention on the Internet.

Turkle is convinced that "life on the screen" is something very new and different. Online technology now "links millions of people in new spaces that are changing the way we think, the nature of our sexuality, the form of our communities, our very identities" (9). We have stepped through the looking glass and are inventing ourselves as we go along in the exploration of real and virtually real worlds. *Life on the Screen* validates the experiences of cyberexplorers as a worthwhile component of the voyage of self-realization through intense relationships on the Internet.

Turkle develops her thesis by exploring three main ideas in *Life on the Screen* from which she derives the notion that the traditional distance between people and machines has become harder to maintain. Turkle eschews the popular analogy of the computer's holding power described in language associated with drugs ("user") in favor of a metaphor of seduction that cleverly emphasizes the attraction between the person and the machine. Turkle then provides concrete examples of how people modify their experiences with computers in a way that each machine becomes a Rorschach test, open to interpretation and operating as a launching point for ideas. Programmers, for example, experience a sense of union with the technology when they construct personal knowledge systems in the computer, knowledge systems that they are then able to see and interact with.

Influenced by French postmodernist thinkers such as Jacques Lacan and Michel Foucault, whose ideas she first encountered while a student in Paris during the late 1960s and early 1970s, Turkle is acutely aware of how computers are redefining us on both an individual and a cultural level. Despite her early training, it was not until she experienced life in cyberspace many years later that these ideas crystallized for her. Turkle explains how modernism, which has dominated Western thinking since the Enlightenment, is characterized by such terms as *linear, logical,* and *hierarchical.* Postmodernism, described as *decentered, fluid, nonlinear,* and *opaque,* is a philosophy that has confused many, including Turkle, until her experiences with computers and cyberspace made the theory tangible. In Part 1, Turkle looks at the computer as machine and "the diversity of forces that keeps us engrossed in computational media" (30). More specifically, Turkle describes Multiple-User Domains (MUDs) through which people have been able to experience a decentered postmodern philosophy. MUDs put you and other MUD players in virtual spaces where you interact through written text via a central computer where the text and program are housed. MUD characters talk, argue, sleep, flirt, and "experience" other aspects of life — all online and in cyberspace.

In MUDs, players are identified only by the name of the character or characters they create. This anonymity gives players "the chance to express multiple and often unexplored aspects of the self, to play with their identity and to try out new ones" (12). MUDs make possible the "creation of an identity so fluid and multiple that it strains the limits of the notion" (12). Turkle vividly captures players' fascination with their cyberspace experiences and how the distinction between real life (RL) and a series of virtual worlds becomes blurred for many of them. Some players challenge the idea of giving RL priority. After all, according to one MUD user, "Why grant such superior status to the self that has

the body, when the selves that don't have bodies are able to have different kinds
of experiences?" (14). Turkle's accounts of MUD players offer great insight into
the psychology of a computer culture that no longer sees the computer as merely
a machine that works for us but as one that works through us and extends our
physical presence. This in turn raises important questions about our search for
identity in a postmodern society. In a social foundations context, this idea has
particular bearing on curriculum theorists, who only recently have begun to look
at the implications of virtual technologies and their impact on curriculum content, its delivery, and their effect on the user. Has the machine become the self?
Turkle sums up the cultural shift by saying that we are moving from a modernist
culture of calculation toward a postmodernist culture of simulation, navigation,
and interaction in which "your identity on the computer is the sum of your distributed presence" (13). According to Turkle, these new relations based on technology force us to consider to what extent we ourselves have become cyborgs,
transgressive mixtures of biology, technology, and code.

In Part 2, Turkle develops the idea of the machine's "intelligence" and proposes
that although the computer is not alive, it has a "psychology" much like a person.
In interviews with children in the late 1980s, Turkle observed that children interacting with computers for the first time had difficulty deciding whether or not
computers were alive. Nearly ten years later, Turkle found significant differences—children drew a clear boundary between that which is alive and a machine.
However, what children saw on the other side of that line had drastically changed.
Children's perceptions of computers included qualities previously reserved for humans, thus blurring the distinction between machine and person. Turkle observed
that computers were seen as having intentions and ideas, acting as partners for dialogue and relations, and possessing other human attributes. These observations of
children mirror a societal change in the perceptions of computers that are now seen
"less like a traditional machine and more like a demi-person" (85). Turkle raises
complex questions about humans and their interactions with computers— questions that humankind must analyze vis à vis the emergence of new virtual
technologies.

Finally, Turkle addresses the notion of a dynamic, multidimensional self,
evolving in light of the relationships built with and through the computer. Turkle's
most insightful argument is her psychological analysis of the IBM/Mac debate,
which she defines in terms of "hard" and "soft" models of computing. She sees the
IBM format, a hard model, as catering to those who don't mind the feeling of "virtual dirt" on their hands, those who like to know their systems inside out and feel
comfortable with rule-driven computing. In the soft model of computing,
Macintosh loyalists tend to work in ignorance of the underlying mechanism and
rules. However, this encourages learning through exploration, and interaction is
encouraged with the Macintosh because the foreboding technical workings of the
machine are neatly hidden underneath the simulated desktop. Turkle uses the term

bricolage or *tinkering* to define an approach to computing in which experimentation is seen as part of the learning process in thinking through problems. She believes "bricoleurs approach problem solving by entering into a relation with their work materials that has more the flavor of a conversation than a monologue" (51). It is the idea of having a conversation with technology that leads to the redefinition of our relation with computers. Turkle echoes the belief of other writers in the field of computers and culture that the Macintosh operating system allowed many to interact with technology in ways believed to be reserved only for traditional academics and programmers.

Turkle uses the image of tinkering to deftly argue that computer windows have become a powerful metaphor for thinking about the self as a multiple distributed system. Just as we handle different tasks on multiple screens, our identity operates on different levels when using a computer. Turkle argues that on the Internet, people are able to "build a self by cycling through many selves" (178). Although in the past, having different identities was tantamount to being on the fringe of society, it is not so in the postmodern era, argues Turkle. She writes, "Many more people experience identity as a set of roles that can be mixed and matched, whose diverse demands need to be negotiated" (180). Experiences in cyberspace, according to Turkle, encourage us to discover and find a new way to talk about psychological health not in terms of constructing one but of negotiating many.

In *Life on the Screen,* Turkle carefully develops her arguments, allowing the reader to synthesize her insightful blend of psychological and philosophical analysis of the Internet with personal anecdotes from her participants. It is through her case studies in particular that we are forced to ask if we are living on the screen or in the screen as a result of the new realities we create and in which we immerse ourselves. Personal computers, MUDs, and the Internet become objects-to-think-with for the postmodern era, Turkle writes, much like the idea of the Freudian slip of the previous century that helped people deal with the notion that we had a darker side to our personalities. Virtual worlds are merely tools for understanding the changes computers are inducing in our minds and selves. Turkle has redefined Freud for postmodern times and presents us with the challenge to understand and use our virtual experiences to enrich the real —an idea that must be actively incorporated in the emerging computing philosophy. The lasting importance of Turkle's work is this reinterpretation of psychoanalysis for the twenty-first century. Yet, in the process of creating the multidimensional self, is it now acceptable to cast off identities and assume new ones just as easily? On the surface, Turkle's case studies would indicate that in expanding the self we are, in fact, relinquishing that which defines us as individuals. Turkle's parallels between the psychoanalysis of old and simulation of today, however, encourage just the opposite. If the computer is a reflection of humankind, indeed a second self, then the culture of simulations warrants further analysis because navigating in virtual worlds demands self-reflection and self-monitoring to ensure that the self is not lost in these cyberwanderings. Turkle issues a timely call for continuing the practical study of self-knowledge "as we struggle to make meaning from our lives on the screen" (269).

Reference

Turkle, Sherry. 1984. *The Second Self.* New York: Simon & Schuster.

Literacy Online: The Promise (and Peril) of Reading and Writing with Computers. Myron C. Tuman. Pittsburgh: University of Pittsburgh Press, 1992. pp. 284. $49.95.

ELIZABETH D. CRAMER
University of Miami

Computers and related technologies have indisputably affected contemporary literacy. By way of providing new forms of texts, new forms of teaching English, as well as altering the ease of administrative control and the spreading of information and material, information is no longer shared in the same way. Although literacy debates were popular throughout the 1980s, the direction of these debates changed in the 1990s due to the increasing influence that computers have had on the issue.

Literacy Online is the outgrowth of a symposium on American literature held at the University of Alabama in the fall of 1989. Essays on the subject of literacy and computers were presented by some of the country's leading experts in literature, technology, and education. The book, edited by Myron Tuman, is a compilation of the papers presented at the conference as well as discussions of their meaning and content.

Tuman opens the book with his thoughts on the ways that technology has revolutionized how modern society interacts with literacy. He then outlines the views of the authors whose essays became chapters of the book, discussing the impact that computers have on literacy from the perspective of their field of expertise. The chapters are divided into five sections: "Computers and New Forms of Texts," "Computers and New Forms of Teaching English," "Computers and New Forms of Critical Thought," "Computers and New Forms of Administrative Control," and "Computers and New Forms of Knowledge."

The first of the book's authors is Jay David Bolter, who writes of "Literature in the Electronic Writing Space." He discusses hypertext and the new model of book, the "electronic book." A sample electronic book is described and the reader is shown how a story can be so different and "textured" when one is able to interact with it, to make decisions about it, and to make changes to the material that is presented. He also points out the need for repetition in text when such changes are occurring. He best describes this new form of reading and writing when he states, "In electronic writing, reader and the author share in the act of making the text and therefore in the responsibility for the result" (31). He does recognize the threats that this poses to the tradition of literature, yet he still sees interactive literature as "an exciting process because it places our work with computers and writing at the center of the computer revolution" (42).

The theme of hypertext continues in the essay of Theodor Holm Nelson entitled, "Opening Hypertext." He discusses the three possibilities that hypertext brings to the writing process: branching literature; organizing, visualizing, and intercomparing ideas; and constructs. He also discusses the Xanadu system, an experimental hypertext publishing system, and the direction in which it would be changing due to hypertext.

The hypertext issue is also relevant in a discussion about new forms of teaching English. George Landow writes about "Hypertext, Metatext, and the Electronic Canon." Landow describes the way in which novels can be explored and linked through hypertext. He also shares an idea for using metatext for the linking of fields for interdisciplinary study. Finally, he discusses the literary canon (the inner circle of elite literature) and how computers can expand this canon to include works that may not have otherwise been noted. Computers enable teachers to introduce works from women and minorities more easily by facilitating the process of obtaining such materials and by linking these works to more traditional ones.

In "Computers as Cultural Artifacts," by Helen Schwartz, computers are described as "agents of human culture." She discusses the perils of computer use such as the modification of reality to enforce theories, the way in which computers are more cognitive than cultural, and their fallibility due to humans. She also reviews her own software program, "SEEN," which includes idea-generating tutorials and idea-sharing bulletin boards. Finally, she discusses hypertext as a prosthesis for the reader and writer "because it can integrate the right-brained experience of graphics and the left-brained analysis of language" (106).

In the third section, Stanley Aronowitz writes on "The Impact of Computers on the Lives of Professionals." Aronowitz describes the ways in which a computer can be used as a teacher, tool, tutor, and an output for technology. He describes the technoculture, which is defined as the intertwining of culture with technology.

Gregory L. Ulmer adds to this discussion with "Grammatology (in the Stacks) of Hypermedia, a Simulation: Or, when does a pile become a heap?" He illustrates examples of hypertext by linking a series of quotations from various works of literature through stacks. Ulmer claims that his essay is similar to Aronowitz's in that they both discuss the adjustments that institutions and individuals must make in the face of technology as well as the idea of the involvement of human cognition and logic in this process.

In the fourth section, "The Electronic Panopticon: Censorship, Control, and Indoctrination in a Post-Typographic Culture," Eugene F. Provenzo, Jr., points out the potential perils that computer use may encourage in our society. He sees this as a potential normalization tool drawing on the work of the French social theorist Michel Foucault (1979). He also illustrates examples of companies keeping track of consumer habits through the use of computers and compares this phenomenon to Orwell's *1984*. Provenzo goes on to recognize threats such as the changing of history and fact by digitally altering photographs or recorded data by the click of the mouse or the stroke of a key. He sums up his thoughts about technology by contending that "it is a powerful tool for creativity and productivity. But it is a tool that, if we do not control its use, will allow others to control us, and in doing so destroy the foundations of our democratic society" (187).

Victor Raskin discusses natural language interfaces and computers and cultural literacy in his piece, "Naturalizing the Computer: English Online." He looks at the different systems under which computers operate and stresses the point that consumers are looking for the most friendly types of software. He shares many of Provenzo's views on the potential dangers computer use may lead to but defends computers by saying that anything that is a threat due to computers is also a threat in some way regardless of computers.

In the final section of the book, Richard Lanham's "Digital Rhetoric: Theory, Practice, and Property" examines the way in which computers enable us to make the font resemble the message. Also, the use of icons in general is seen as a way to expand the understanding of literature. He considers this "the means of digital expression [that] prove[s] to be a fulfillment, not only of postmodern aesthetic but also of a larger phenomenon that comprehends and explains the aesthetic. ..." (243).

Pamela McCorduck writes the final essay in the work, "How We Knew, How We Know, How We Will Know." She takes a historical approach to viewing the way the communication of information has changed over the years, beginning with prehistoric art and ending with the use of computers to seek information for the future.

The book's editor, Myron Tuman, offers practical advice at the close of the book but recognizes that the computer world is constantly changing. He acknowledges the possibility that books may become obsolete. He expresses this notion not with concern but with the suggestion that perhaps this generation is the last to be concerned if books exist. He sees *Literacy Online* as "a time-capsule preserving for future students of literacy a record of what thinkers, so successfully acculturated into print culture, had to say about the profound impact ... that ... computers are about to have on our practice of reading and writing" (269).

Since *Literacy Online* was published seven years ago, compiling essays that were first presented nearly ten years ago, this last comment may have already been realized. Computers are now affecting our practice of reading and writing, yet the ideas brought forth by these authors are still issues of current concern. Even with the dramatic technological improvements that have taken place over the last decade, the questions these authors posed in the late 1980s remain largely unanswered today.

These collected essays, along with the interesting discussions that follow each major section, offer insights according to a variety of viewpoints and areas of expertise on the subject of computers and literacy. The relevance of the work increases as does the application and use of computers in the schools.

Reference

Foucault, Michel. 1979. *Discipline and Punish*. Translated by Alan Sheridan. New York: Random House.

The Gutenberg Elegies: The Fate of Reading in an Electronic Age. Sven Birkerts. New York: Fawcett Columbine, 1994. pp. 231.

ELIZABETH D. CRAMER
University of Miami

With the rapid growth and development of technology in the past few decades, the way in which Americans work, communicate, and learn has been radically redefined. The computer has become a fundamental part of the work, education, and leisure of most people. This proliferation of technology comes at a price. As Robert Coover wrote in an important essay published in the *New York Times Book Review* (1992), "The End of Books," "In the real world nowadays ... the print medium is a doomed and outdated technology, a mere curiosity of bygone days and destined soon to be consigned forever to those dusty unattended museums we now call libraries" (24).

Is this true? In *The Gutenberg Elegies*, Sven Birkerts addresses this question by looking at the fate of reading in light of the new technologies like computers that have increasingly taken the place of books and other printed medium in recent years. As an author of three books of literary criticism and numerous reviews and essays, as well as a former manager of a bookstore, Birkerts has a real concern for the possible extinction of the printed form. Through an examination of his love of literature and reading, he shows his concern for the fate of reading as an art and human concern.

In Part 1 of the book, Birkerts first examines the concept of the individual as a reader. Through the vehicle of an autobiographical chapter, he examines how reading became a crucial aspect of his life. He portrays the act of reading as an art form, as a means of escaping the troubles of reality, as a process that shapes the individual as a whole, and as a cultural experience that molds the society as a collective group.

In Part 2, he addresses the technological improvements that have taken place as we approach what he labels "The Electronic Millennium." He addresses the fundamental differences in the reader's focus and comprehension with the print medium versus electronic forms such as hypermedia and hypertext. In an electronic context, information travels along a network. It is no longer necessarily linear, the pace is rapid, and the content is often linked. Rather than running on a continuum, information comes in spurts, often at the click of a button. Through hypertext, reading and writing become interactive. Reader and writer become what Coover (1992) described as "co-learners or cowriters." Birkerts argues that the use of hypertext and hypermedia changes the nature of the written word from permanent to a transformable and mutable form. He argues that this has changed the process of writing and therefore reading as a whole.

In Part 3, the final part of the book, Birkerts addresses the potential dangers of the influx of technology at the expense of the process of reading as we know it. He compares the effect of modern technology on communication, and in turn, on reading, to Gutenberg's invention of movable type. He predicts that "ten, fifteen years from now the world will be nothing like what we remember, nothing much like we experience now. We will still wear clothes and live in dwellings, but our relation to the space–time axis will be very different from what we have lived in for millennia. We will be swimming in impulses and data—the microchip will make us offers that will be very hard to refuse. And the old, solid, dense, obstacle-ridden world that we know from historical legend (or if we are old enough, from our youth) will recede into memory" (193).

He also predicts that time as a whole will shift and that we will be living in the "virtual now" or "cybertime."

Birkerts does not view technology as a completely negative influence on the future of humanity. Rather he realizes its potential to reshape the ways in which we live and work. He states this point of view quite eloquently when he remarks, "Yes, I've been to the crossroads and I've met the devil, and he's sleek and confident, ever so much more 'with it' than the nearest archangel....He is the sorcerer of the binary order, jacking in and out of terminals, booting up, flaming, commanding vast systems and networks with an ease that steals my breath away. I don't hate him—I admire and fear him...." (229). He understands the power of the new technology and the potential influence that it has to shape society as we know it.

Birkerts is influenced in his interpretation by various authors and their works, including Robert Coover, Alvin Kernan's *Death of Literature* (1990) and Lionel

Trilling's *The Liberal Imagination* (1950). His perspective is also shaped by his own experience with literature and with technology. In developing his study, he reflects on his own experience listening to books on tapes, working with interactive CD Roms, and surfing the Web. He uses his combination of experiences as an author, a reader, and a cultural voyager to illustrate his understanding of where we've been, where we are, and the "cyberunknown" for which we are headed.

This book provides an interesting perspective on the potential problems and perils of literacy in an electronic age. In the case of the author of this review, someone who like Birkerts has enjoyed the pleasure of stealing away with many novels as well as putting words on paper as a form of expression, nostalgic longing for libraries populated solely by books can be easily understood. However, it is important to realize that the changes that Birkerts predicts are clearly under way and seemingly inevitable. Yet these advancements in technology need not be seen as an end to communication as we know it. Those who can learn to embrace change and do so without losing their fundamental values and priorities may see the electronic future or millennium as a potentially rich culture in which to participate. Ignoring the new literacy seems unlikely in light of the potential possibilities it offers. Birkerts makes us acutely aware of the question of how this new technology should be used to its best advantage and what it is that we lose of the older and more traditional culture through its use.

References

Coover, Robert. 1992. "The End of Books." *New York Times Book Review,* 1(1)(June): 23–25.
Kernan, Alvin. 1990. *The Death of Literature.* New Haven, Conn.: Yale University Press.
Trilling, Lionel. 1950. *The Liberal Imagination.* New York: Harcourt Brace.

Growing Up Digital: The Rise of the Net Generation. Don Tapscott. Washington, D.C.: McGraw-Hill, 1998.

LYDIA C. BARZA
University of Miami

There are 80 million children of the baby boomers. In *Growing Up Digital: The Rise of the Net Generation,* Don Tapscott tries to solve the mystery of what secrets this group holds. In doing so, he finds many clues in the technology they use. Influenced by Neil Postman (1995) and Marshall McLuhan's (1966) idea that "the best way to understand a culture is to examine its tools for conversation," Tapscott ventures into cyberspace to investigate what he describes as the "Net Generation" (63).

Growing Up Digital is a comprehensive overview of what children do with computers and some of the controversies related to their use. Author of *The Digital Economy,* Tapscott acts as a guide through the world of wired adolescents and young adults. He defines Net lingo (like *hacking, flaming, MUDs, c-friend*), addresses problems, and proposes solutions to them.

Tapscott received help from over 300 cybercontributors in writing the book. The great majority of the book is based on an experiment through FreeZone, a monitored Web site for children and young adults between the ages of four and twenty used for chatting and exchanging information. Using the FreeZone Web site as the main source of data for his research, Tapscott interacted with hundreds of young people online for a period of over a year. Participants' impressions are summarized and quotes of their responses to various prompts are provided.

Any understanding of the sociological, psychological, and educational impact of Internet technology cannot be complete without a comparison to the technology of television. The nature of each as a passive (television) versus interactive (Internet) media is explored. Tapscott assumes that the Internet is essentially an interactive medium. One cannot perform operations or make use of it without engaging in constant, active participation and feedback with the computer. Internet use, particularly surfing and chatting, requires the exercise of critical thinking skills and judgment. In contrast, television is a passive medium. Children do not and cannot exert control over television for they are not producers, writers, or directors of programs. However, children can and do control the Internet because they often are producers, writers, and directors of programs. Tapscott argues that the Net Generation prefers the interactive computer screen to the unidirectional nature of television. As evidence of this trend, he notes that "today's kids watch less television than five years ago" (3). One survey found that 92% of children said that the Internet was more fun than television.

Tapscott holds that the Net generation is smarter than the TV generation (99). He says, "Never before has it been more necessary that children learn how to read, write, and think critically" (63). He also credits the interactive environment of the Internet for strengthening "verbal ability and the expression of ideas" (70). Children face the dangers of cyberporn, decide whether Web materials or peers' chatting are authentic, and make choices about relevant information for their searches, sometimes simultaneously on one screen. According to Tapscott, they are developing skills that TV generation kids were not developing at the same age. He argues that "when children control their media, rather than passively observe, they develop faster" (7). Thus, he asserts that the Internet enhances child development.

Even though the social sciences dictate that play is a critical element in human development, Tapscott mocks the idea that "certain segments of society are publicly worried that our children are having too much fun" (160). Some have theorized that the Internet hinders the development of proper social skills. Tapscott argues in contrast that "the same kinds of conversations occur while traveling through the galaxies as happen over the Lego set or the model train" (107). He expands this notion by arguing that "it is not the N-Gen children who are being robbed of social development, it is those adults who, through fear or ignorance, deny themselves the experience of participating in the great revolution of our times" (108).

Tapscott suggests that some characteristics of the Web world actually function to protect children from harm. For example, he maintains that virtually reinventing oneself on the Internet is beneficial. If a child has a bad experience on the Net, he or she may reenter a chat group with a different Net handle (name), thus avoiding the social isolation that might have been imposed in a real, versus virtual, playground setting. As in real life, there are also consequences, such as losing a cyberfriend. Tapscott thus suggests that the anonymity inherent to the Internet can be used as a vehicle to experiment with social situations and perhaps downplays any harmful effects. He equates, but does not adequately address, the discrepancies in how the two worlds function socially. Similarly, on the subject of cybersex, Tapscott suggests that it is a fairly safe venue for adolescents to experiment with their own sexuality and provides examples of what children typically say to each other when thus engaged. He believes that cyberdating is basically a healthy way for adolescents to experiment with romantic relationships. This type of sex is dubbed "safe" given that there is no preoccupation with rape, pregnancy, and sexually transmitted diseases. Because the Internet is an interactive devise that puts the user in control, the child may simply disconnect if anything becomes overwhelming.

Tapscott also explores networked-based learning. "Instructivism," or what Tapscott refers to as broadcast learning, consists of one teacher disseminating the same information to a group of students. In contrast, interactive learning via the Internet may be customized for individual students. He presents an example of a Computer Aided Instruction (CAI) and states that "CAI programs improve learning performance by one-third" although he does not include a discussion about the politics of standardized testing (140). Consistent with a constructivist approach, he suggests that learners be involved in designing curricula. Fostering lifelong learning has perhaps never been so important as it is now. He describes the rapidly changing economy and workforce structures that dictate that one must consistently acquire new skills in order to be employable. Further, once N-Geners understand the importance of lifelong learning, they will demand it from their employers.

Tapscott describes the characteristics of the new teacher as motivator and facilitator rather than fact repeater. Students are urged to take responsibility for their own learning by doing and not just passively listening. Cooperation, seen as increasingly important in the new workforce, should be fostered in the classroom as well. It is important for students to have a meaningful purpose and discover and share their own expertise. This idea is reminiscent of Gardner's (1983) theory of multiple intelligence. The goal is not expertise in everything but identifying personal strengths. The computer is an ideal medium for such interactivity. Nonetheless, access is not enough. Tapscott reveals the common practical problems associated with students working on computers. For example, students who take the bus home promptly after school cannot benefit from computer lab hours or after-school programs.

Tapscott hypothesizes that the control available to an Internet user will produce a generation of consumers who expect the same amount of control, customization, and immediacy in all of their lifestyle choices. The nature of customization is becoming so specified that N-Geners are virtually both consumers and producers. Tapscott uses the example of buying bread from a company that allows you to specify the ingredients you prefer and time of delivery. The customization trend also yields an atmosphere emphasizing relationships between sellers and consumers. Free trials of products before purchasing are becoming common as well.

Tapscott reveals that "ninety-eight percent of corporate America is forecasted to be on the Web in the next two years" (191). Comparison shopping will reach a new level. He discusses the declining influence of brands in attracting sales, because function and value are increasingly emphasized. Tapscott divulges the following formula: "In marketing, interactivity equals increased power to the consumer to make informed choices and to buy products which deliver real benefits and value over those which do not" (196). He talks about the advent of software agents who are like personal assistants who get to know your preferences and may be sent online to select items for you. Thus, he predicts the arrival of digital cash, which may overcome the obstacle many minors have in making purchases on the Net—lack of a credit card.

Children are potentially more knowledgeable about products than their parents because of their mastery of the Net. They may compare prices and consumer reports in a matter of minutes. Tapscott states that "the Net is also changing our perception of children — from being ignorant to competent" (114). He also describes the "generation lap," "kids outpacing and overtaking adults on the technology track" (36). Tapscott believes that this translates into power and more egalitarian relationships in the home. The result will be an atmosphere of mutual respect for each other's authority.

It is suggested that parents' anxieties about the Internet are more about their own discomfort with abdicating control over their children's newfound expressions of autonomy than anything else. According to Tapscott, the first of the ten themes of the N-Gen culture is fierce independence. He accuses the media of "focusing on the 0.5 percent of online material that is violent, racist, or sexual in nature" (44). He also believes that Net addiction is an idea perpetrated by those preaching an antitechnology sentiment. As an example he sites that voracious readers who can by the same standards be technically labeled book addicted are not. He and his 300 collaborators are fiercely against censorship of the Internet. Rather, within every "cybersmart" family's walls there should be discussion about rules concerning online safety. Blocking programs are ineffective because there are always ways around them that children figure out and pass on to each other. Thus, a family's best defense against cyberthreats is open communication: "The open family discusses the issue of inappropriate material and develops a mutually acceptable approach to dealing with it" (252).

Brains triumph over brawn in this new era. Knowledge is capital, thus the traditional hierarchy is doomed. Inept workers can no longer hide behind a title and hope that no one notices their incompetence. Tapscott describes the old command and control hierarchy model in enterprise and shows how it cannot continue to function as it has in the past given the Net generation's commitment to innovation, knowledge, immediacy, and internetworking. He talks of the Net generation's creed of collaboration and knowledge sharing in much the same way that other visionaries in the field talk about collective intelligence. Entrepreneurship is also a part of their creed. An example of a business initiated by persons in their twenties demonstrates how different this generation's view of management is from the traditional hierarchical view. A flat organization style allows businesses to foster employees' entrepreneurial spirit by giving them responsibility and ownership of their ideas rather than suppressing them. The older N-Geners, according to Tapscott, are beginning to experience the frustration of conflicting styles of work within traditional companies.

Tapscott describes a digital divide between computer access and knowledge—the haves and have-nots. Nevertheless, as often occurs throughout the book, he speculates upon a few possible remedies. A symbiotic relationship between schools and businesses is described. Schools benefit from instructional and material donations from businesses and businesses benefit from tax exemptions and the opportunity to hire adept people whom they have trained. Communities may also contribute. He tells of how several community computing networks, nonprofit Internet service providers, are successfully minimizing the digital divide. Tapscott believes that government intervention is an obstacle to progress.

Tapscott's informed predictions of how the new Internet technology will evolve is one of the most engaging aspects of the book. His use of actual online examples from children and young adults make his broader arguments all the more convincing. As an author, he seems to have his finger on the proverbial pulse of techno-savvy children and adolescents. The work is replete with relevant facts, statistics, and graphs that complement his thoughts. A positive hope for the future of the Net generation is clearly expressed. Tapscott also implies that those who do not surf may be swallowed up by the wave. This is a useful work for anyone trying to get a handle on the implications of the Internet for shaping contemporary childhood and youth populations.

References

Gardner, H. 1983. *Frames of Mind: The Theory of Multiple Intelligences.* New York: Basic Books.

McLuhan, Marshall. 1966. *Understanding Media: The Extensions of Man.* Toronto, Ontario, Canada: The New American Library of Canada.

Postman, Neil. 1995. *The End of Education: Redefining the Value of School.* New York: Vintage, 1995.

Points of Viewing Children's Thinking: A Digital Ethnographer's Journey. Ricki Goldman-Segall. Mahwah, N.J.: Lawrence Erlbaum Associates, Inc. 1998. pp. xxvii, 285.

AUBREY CAMPBELL
University of Miami

> Man is most nearly himself when he achieves the seriousness of a child at play.

> *—Heraclitus, Greek philosopher (500 B.C.)*

Ricki Goldman-Segall's *Points of Viewing Children's Thinking: A Digital Ethnographer's Journey* is a study of the ways children play in a multimedia environment. By studying their play, she discovers the diverse ways they think and how they construct their own knowledge through a range of multimedia lenses and associated technologies as well as educational methodological frameworks.

Goldman-Segall's work is a participant observation study of her own work as a multimedia ethnographer—a field that has involved her development of multimedia ethnographic research tools for making sense of video data. In the context of multiple representations, she develops a cutting-edge protocol for freeing children from "traditional teaching" to learn in multiple ways according to their diverse learning styles and to capture, decode, and aggregate these learning events in different ways.

Goldman-Segall describes her book as a "longitudinal multimedia ethnographic study" (available online: http://www.merlin.ubc.ca/people/ricki/) at two schools: Bayside Middle School on Vancouver Island, British Columbia, and Hennigan Elementary School in New England. Essentially, the book juxtaposes the case studies of these two apparently different schools, allowing for varied means of data analysis.

In her preface, Goldman-Segall describes the book as "a living narrative — an evolving story told with words, moving images, and sounds" (ix). She further ascribes the "thick descriptions" (à la Clifford Geertz 1973) of children's thinking in the book to her learning during her interdisciplinary doctoral work under the supervision of Seymour Papert (available online: http://www.merlin.ubc.ca/people/ricki/). From this she creates an excellent book that derives its interactivity from embedded hyperlinks. These hyperlinked videoclips, and an interactive contributor's site online at http: www.pointsofviewing.com, combine to "thicken" the narrative text and bring the book to virtual life. A Web reporter calls Goldman-Segall's book a book/Web site. As such, it represents one of the new directions in publishing being created as a result of the Internet and World Wide Web (i.e., the Web-supported book).

Goldman-Segall's learning model rests upon a reappraisal of Piaget's (1970) theory of learning stages and Papert's theory of learning styles. The creative way she uses this new medium to represent reality develops from her close encounters with the children at the two study sites. She proposes a theory of epistemological pluralism and views learning as layers of knowledge structures that deepen one's experiences in both real and virtual ways. For Goldman-Segall, diverse users interpret selected recordings and field notes, infusing multiple layers of interpretations into the database. In essence, the book/Web site puts her theory of methodological pluralism into practice by facilitating the construction of an enriched, growing body of interpretations of reader/viewer experiences.

On her Web site, Goldman-Segall also puts forward her notion of Advanced Cognitive Technologies, carried in the construction of an interactive book/Web site using video and computer technologies to explore issues that touch young people's lives. Through current or actuality issues, each student learns and develops and constructs his or her own knowledge schema pertaining to the issues they put forward.

Goldman-Segall further examines the culture arising from the educational use of technology and designing ethnographic methods using digital tools to explore children's thinking. Video is the primary research tool Goldman-Segall uses to catch children's candid, often insightful ideas when using computers and media technologies as expressive forms. Her book and Web site complement each other as readers view the video of the children online, while readers themselves participate in online discussions.

From her research, Goldman-Segall discovers how electronic media can work in tandem with authentic learning experiences connected to the real world. Bayside students studied and completed projects about the endangered rain forest (Clayoquot Sound) using video, the Web, and image manipulation programs. They construct their own curriculum, learning things that interest them. Technology connected to issues children feel strongly about is a new facet in learning. The children tell their own stories through multimedia. Learning becomes their living and they live their learning. In an interview, Goldman-Segall said, "I'm interested in making it so it's not like all the stuff is coming *at* the kid but rather that the kid is doing something that goes back out into the culture and so then she or he is participating in the making of culture."

Goldman-Segall's central metaphor for children's thinking is one of stories, supported by videoclips, where children capture and share their own experiences, their own stories, in print and audiovisual media, rather than listen to those of teachers. For her, children's own stories reveal the way they think. If teachers are to help children learn better about their world, children need help to tell their own stories. From these stories, teachers will learn how children learn and learn along with them.

Versatility and flexibility, two crucial characteristics of digital multimedia, arise as issues in Goldman-Segall's book. Being versatile, computers already emulate books, audiocassettes, CD and digital video disk players, video games, TVs, telephones, VCRs, spreadsheets, drafting tables, editing studios, or even battlefields, ecosystems, and weather systems. With computers, teachers can control and combine many of these separate learning tools to create hybrids of greater learning and teaching power. Computers can help create books that talk, a voice that types, a database that dials the telephone and manages finances, a video with an audio and a text track, a virtual reality.

The flexibility of multimedia helps teachers learn about the various strengths and limitations of children's sensory, motor, motivational, and emotional makeup; in short, most of their entire life world. Countering the "one size fits all" of traditional teaching, digital media are malleable, adjustable, and adaptable for different learners.

Goldman-Segall's book makes a strong case for using multimedia in learning materials and activities that can increase access for learners with wide disparities in their abilities to experience the world and make sense of these experiences. Therefore, stakeholders in curriculum design face significant challenges in improving and applying the principles of multimedia interactive design. Curricula that meet the needs of the most challenged students and those with the highest learning goals will better serve all learners. Creating such flexible curricula has potential to address crucial ethical issues of equity and equal access to learning opportunities. Multimedia in curriculum design provides this vast potential for creating educational materials with ample width, depth, and flexibility to reach all learners and learning contexts effectively.

Goldman-Segall's unique contribution involves not only her expanded understanding of the potential role of multimedia in cognition and learning but also her highly innovative use of technology in the creation of her book and accompanying Web site. This is a highly innovative work that represents a precedent setting study in the field and suggests not only some of the new models of technology and education but also some of the new models of scholarship and writing we will increasingly see in the future.

References

Geertz, Clifford. 1973. *The Interpretation of Cultures.* New York: Basic Books.
Piaget, J. 1970. *Genetic Epistemology.* Translated by E. E. Duckworth. New York: Norton.

The Children's Machine: Rethinking School in the Age of the Computer. Seymour Papert. New York: HarperCollins, 1992. pp. 241.

PHILOMENA MARINACCIO
University of Miami

Seymour Papert is the creator of the computer language Logo and a professor at Massachusetts Institute of Technology. In *The Children's Machine: Rethinking in the Age of the Computer,* he presents a series of challenging concepts about the connection between computers and educational reform. He believes that the *megachange* brought about as a result of the use of computers in education will profoundly challenge not only how, but what, schools teach in the future.

Papert contends that theoretical and pragmatic obstacles that have hindered past attempts at evolving theory into practice in education can be remedied through the use of technology. We are introduced to his theories of epistemology and technology through three themes: what is happening in schools, a new learning theory, and by developing a better sense of the evolution of technology.

According to Papert, one of the biggest threats to change in the classroom concerns the issue of control. He blames schools for reducing learning to a series of technical bits in order to alienate the child from what is being learned. In this way schools and teachers control learning. The *knowledge machine* in the classroom has the power to put what others know into the hands of the student. However, schools have mechanisms similar to immune reactions to defend against change. Papert's solution to help children regain control of their own learning is to recapture the child's natural love of learning.

Papert also believes that the traditional curriculum falls short of recognizing the importance of concrete thinking as an avenue for learning. "A central theme of my message is that a prevailing tendency to overvalue abstract reasoning is a major obstacle to progress in education" (137). Papert's proposed theory of learning differs from traditional pedagogy by its emphasis on discovery learning, learning from failure, allowing time for learning to blossom, and intuitive understanding.

Papert's second theme involves a new theory of learning that focuses on how knowledge is acquired. He recognizes that his constructivist approach is not new and speaks with reverence and genuine admiration when referring to theorists such as Piaget, Vygotsky, and Dewey. At the same time Papert acknowledges that pre-

vious attempts to assimilate theory into practice have been short-lived, and because of pragmatic concerns, have a tendency to return to traditional teaching
practices. Even Dewey, when faced with the impossibility of having one teacher
responsible for teaching across the curriculum, returned to departmentalization.

Papert's solution to these pragmatic and theoretical obstacles to reform is the
use of technology. The pragmatic concern of meeting the specialized needs of a diverse group of students is possible through the use of the computer because "the
powerful contribution of the new technologies in the enhancement of learning is
the creation of personal media capable of supporting a wide range of intellectual
styles" (ix). Similarly, the computer satisfies constructivist pedagogy by allowing
children to manipulate and explore environments through computer programming
such as Logo and simulations such as *microworlds*.

Finally, in his third theme, Papert provides systematic strategies for implementing change such as utilizing *little schools*. He believes that undertaking
megachange is difficult enough without the complications and bureaucracy of
large schools. Through little schools parents and students are given the means of
achieving megachange.

Papert's theory is so inclusive that it is difficult to find limitations in the presentation of his message. He engages us in the contradictions of the traditional curriculum and encourages us to bring about megachange. Although I support Papert's
contention for change, I caution against several of his approaches. It is my opinion
that the computer does provide a wonderful scaffold for children's early attempts
at learning. However, it should not be thought of as a replacement for the dialogic
interaction between a student and a teacher. Experiences that promote social cognition with the teacher and among peers need to remain the basis of a child's learning. My other concern is that microworlds are not entirely authentic or real
environment activities for children. Although they do provide a virtual reality that
allows for exploration of an environment, children need hands-on and tactile activities to complement this technology. Also, in respect to microworlds and simulations, children are not making their own discoveries. Rather they are exploring
environments set up with causal relations that were programmed by someone else.
In this way, learning is still controlled by someone other than the student and does
not allow for the synergistic interrelations a child would experience in exploring
his or her own interests.

My greatest unease, after reading *The Children's Machine,* is in respect to the
use of little schools as an avenue to introduce megachange. I feel that, like
microworlds, little schools are sterile and removed from reality and do not take
into consideration all the possible variables that affect learning. I caution against
the creation of little schools primarily because I believe they are not democratic.
To create specialized schools is potentially divisionary, especially if the opportunity to attend is not available on an equal basis to all. Also, little schools duplicate
rather than learn from the failures of past theory implementation that also lacked

consideration of pragmatic concerns. Dewey's laboratory school was similar to a little school in that it was also an alternative to traditional education, but it failed because of its inability to be transferred effectively into a broader public school context.

This is not to deny the value of much of what Papert proposes. I believe the contribution of *The Learning Machine* to education is best summarized in the following quote: "One really important computer skill is the habit of using the computer in doing whatever one is doing" (51). In the same way that a child learns to read by reading and to write by writing, a child should learn to use the computer by utilizing its capabilities in all aspects of learning. A more detailed examination of this question on the part of Papert would ultimately make this a more valuable contribution to the field.

Writing Space: The Computer, Hypertext, and the History of Writing. Jay David Bolter. Hillsdale, N.J.: Lawrence Erlbaum Associates, Inc. 1991. pp. 240.

ELLEN EMERSON BROWN
University of Miami

Jay David Bolter in *Writing Space: The Computer, Hypertext, and the History of Writing* conducts an engaging inquiry about the computer and its impact on writing. Bolter's thesis is that electronic text, with its unique features including the potential for interactivity and hyperlinking, will replace traditional text. In doing so, the canonical nature of the traditional text is challenged. Hierarchical structures are also replaced, as the authoritative or definitive text gives way to the new electronic forms that provide the reader with a network of multivocal, nonstandardized messages.

In conveying these ideas, new means of writing made possible by the computer change the very nature of "the writing space." Specifically, hypertext (the electronic linking of text to other sources) frees the writer to present ideas through association rather than through more hierarchical structures. Bolter sees this as a radical departure from traditional forms of text. According to him, cultural literacy is not the acquisition of traditional text but rather "access to the vocabulary to read and write effectively" (237).

In Part 1 of *Writing Space,* the reader learns that the computer, as a technology of reading and writing, takes its place as the fourth great medium beside the ancient papyrus scroll, the medieval codex, and the printed book. Bolter contrasts the electronic book with these earlier technologies, maintaining that whereas the printed book is one in which writing is "stable, monumental and controlled exclusively by the author" (11), the conceptual space of electronic writing is characterized by change and an interactive relationship between the reader and the writer.

Electronic writing has a spatial character that also differs from the linear media of text. The Greek word *Topos,* for example, literally means "place," and this in turn reinforces the spatial character of electronic writing. Topics, in this context, exist not only as part of a visual surface but also as part of the data structure found in the computer. Bolter provides a useful representation of topical writing in the conventional outline that turns the writing surface into a tiered space representing the hierarchy of the author's ideas.

What Bolter is trying to communicate in this context is the extent to which writing has changed from a one-dimensional linear process to a multilayered form with complex connections and links. This idea can be seen in Bolter's example of an outline processor. This is a type of program that sets the traditional written outline in motion, revealing or hiding detail as the writer requires. Another programming structure, the "tree," also represents hierarchical structures that record large amounts of information that change frequently. Bolter believes that both the tree and the outline give the reader a better awareness of structure than ordinary paragraphing. Whereas the printed page of paragraphs is "a flat and uninteresting space" (20), the electronic writing space is mutable and changing. The writer may choose to maintain three outlines for instance and examine topics from any of the three vantage points provided and then switch among them. "The writing space itself," says Bolter, "has become a tree, a hierarchy of topical elements" (21).

In this process, Bolter asserts the need for a further step to liberate the text from the necessary subordination of selected topics in a strict hierarchy. He maintains that it is the ability to create and present hypertextual structures that makes the computer a revolution in writing. A network of embedded notes, hypertext is retrieved when the reader points with the cursor at text in boldface and reveals a window, which presents a new paragraph for the reader to consider. According to Bolter, hypertext "gives visual expression to our acts of conceiving and manipulating topics " (17), and thus by allowing the writer to organize by association, it represents a radical departure from traditional writing. As Bolter explains, "The hierarchy (in the form of paragraphs, sections, and chapters) is an attempt to impose order on verbal ideas that are always prone to subvert that order. The associative relationships define alternative organizations that lie beneath the order of pages and chapters that a printed text presents to the world. These alternatives constitute subversive texts-behind-the-text" (22).

Earlier writing technologies such as the papyrus roll with its linear text tended to ignore such alternatives. The medieval codex and then the printed book accommodated association by the index, which permitted the reader to associate passages that were widely separated by the pages of the book. Ultimately, the electronic medium and the new writing space it makes possible accommodate both hierarchical and associative thinking in the structure of the text. Bolter makes clear to the reader that this is significant because "a hypertext has no canonical order. Every path defines an equally convincing and appropriate reading, and in that simple fact the reader's relationship to the text changes radically. A text as a network has no univocal sense; it is multiplicity without the imposition of a principle of domination" (25).

Bolter continues his argument by taking the reader through an informative history of writing from the use of pictures to alphabetic, syllabic, and word signs as visual images of spoken language. He informs the reader that all systems of phonetic writing are analytic and divide the flow of spoken language into a sequence of signs. As the units became fewer, the division became less intuitive and more technical. He elaborates, "Word symbols are units of sound and meaning. Syllables are units of sound only, but they are still sounds that we can hear in isolation. Alphabetic symbols stand for sounds that in general do not occur in isolation: the alphabet is therefore the most abstract system of all, the system farthest removed from a speaker's immediate intuitive knowledge of his or her language" (49).

This passage resonates with anyone who teaches children to read and write. It argues well for explicit instruction in sound-symbol correspondence for beginning readers. But Bolter's point is that although sound replaced the image in the history of writing, the letters continue to influence the reader as visual images. Phonetic principles completely reformed the writing space. Picture writing survived only in religious symbols and heraldry or in trademarks, road signs, and public warning signs that are designed to identify an object rather than convey a message. The computer is special, however, because it combines alphabetic writing with images and diagrams. Thus it creates a writing that is both intuitive and highly abstract. When the computer user reorganizes and activates icons, he or she is writing in the same sense as putting alphabetic characters in a row. According to Bolter, the action that the icon performs is its meaning. Icons function to show how documents are grouped and connected to the program. Bolter compares the use of icons to old Ojibwa picture writing in which the spatial relation between the images is significant to their meaning and not just a convenience of spacing.

Bolter also introduces us to the idea that some picture writing did not require any material surface. A mnemonic system used by the Greeks was one such example. Called the "Art of Memory," the mnemonic system consisted of establishing vivid images in the mind that were "visual equivalents of ideas or names to be remembered. The practitioner of the art then imagined a building or a garden and put vivid images down in it. To recall the images and associated ideas, one imagined oneself walking through the building in a predetermined order and examining each image as it appeared" (57).

Greek and Roman orators delivered long speeches without notes using this type of mnemonic system. Bolter draws a comparison between this art of memory and electronic writing when he claims that electronic writing is the art of encompassing ideas and setting them down in a writing space. For him, this is a topical process and encourages the writer to write with units different from the individual word. Oral literature requires a technical attitude toward performance that he describes as "a sense of difference from everyday speech"(57). In the case of a poet like Homer, a work was created by constructing formulaic blocks that, in turn, were "read" by the audience. Metaphors and key repeated phrases provided the elements that made possible the creation and performance of the mythological stories. Listeners built up networks of associations by hearing these phrases again and again. Just as the early Greek audiences constructed associations around the mythological characters, so electronic readers rely on an interplay between the author's text and their own associative structures.

In Part 2 Bolter discusses the "Conceptual Writing Space" in chapters on the electronic book and the electronic encyclopedia. He also discusses interactive fiction and describes an actual example of the genre that combines a sophisticated story with a computerized adventure game. In this type of fiction, "There is no single story," he writes, "because each reading determines the story as it goes" (124). The last chapter in Part 2, "Critical Theory and the New Writing Space," praises the electronic text for its potential to be participated in and experienced by the reader. According to Bolter, "The computer now extends the role of performer or interpreter to all forms of writing" (158). Whereas the printed book encouraged the making of a canon because it could survive for centuries, and it distanced the author by providing him or her with a writing space not available to most other literate people, the electronic writing space, by contrast, combines two subjects in the text: the writer and the reader. Bolter proclaims this combination as the end of authority. In doing so, he directs the reader to the literary critic and art historian George P. Landow (1989) for a discussion of the way in which literary theories will necessarily change in response to this supposed revolution in writing.

Part 3 of *Writing Space* begins with a chapter on artificial intelligence and goes on to discuss electronic signs and "Writing the Mind." In these chapters Bolter further distinguishes the difference between printing and the electronic text. Whereas printing emphasizes stability, electronic text is mutable and can change each time it is read: "The persona of the text is neither stable nor unified" (213). This again calls for a new theory of literature that Bolter believes may achieve a balance between author, reader, and text.

In the final chapter of *Writing Space,* Bolter contemplates the perils and the promise of computers. In comparing the visual space of the computer to those of the printed word, Bolter laments the degeneration of the quality of typography and graphics. The electronic space is coarser because the pixels define a space inherently different from that of the printed page. Although he expects this situation to improve as computer technology advances and pixels grow smaller and create a denser space, he notes there will be a tension between the character of the electronic writing space and the visual space created by the printed text.

More important than the graphical issues outlined here, Bolter wonders if computer literacy will be universal or limited to an elite, splitting our society into a technology-driven upper class versus a lower class without computer access and skills. Also, he cautions against the use of simulated environments, in museums for instance, when they exclude symbolic systems, or written and mathematical texts. When these are eliminated, a museum becomes no more than a theme park. Finally, he believes, cultural literacy is synonymous with computer literacy.

Bolter's *Writing Space* provides a valuable contribution to the understanding of the potential of computers to shape literacy. His grounding as a scholar in classical Greek and Roman literature, combined with a thorough technical knowledge of the computer, makes Bolter eminently suited to speculate about electronic text and its effect on the culture that embraces it. But although Bolter's comparison of the electronic writer to the ancient storyteller is compelling, I question his assertion that this interchange signals the end of authority. Although it is true that there is flexibility to the storyteller's narrative, it is the consistencies that are of primary interest to the audience. One of the assumptions of the comparative folklorist, for instance, is that a tale that has been found in hundreds of oral variants must have originated in one time and one place by an act of conscious invention. Implicit in this assumption is the idea of an original text or archetype. It is the unchanging units of meaning that elicits the readers' interest, not the multiple variations. If this is true, it does not necessarily follow that the computer will negate the ideal of cultural cohesion or hierarchy. Instead, I would urge Bolter to use his considerable powers of persuasion to recognize and celebrate the significant role electronic text shares with all its forerunners: that of preserving the elements in our culture that have been and continue to be worth transmitting to future generations.

Reference

Landow, George P. 1989. "Hypertext in Literary Education, Criticism, and Scholarship." *Computers and the Humanities* 23: 173–198.

Technopoly: The Surrender of Culture to Technology.

Neil Postman. New York: Vintage, 1992. pp. x, 222.

MICHELE C. MITS CASH
University of Miami

In *Technopoly: The Surrender of Culture to Technology,* Neil Postman chronicles the evolution of society as a tool-using culture and the inevitable ascension of technology over society. He points out that the glut of technologically generated information cannot be harnessed or organized efficiently. He asserts that the sum total of stored information is incommensurate as a collective body of knowledge for any purpose. Yet, as a society we tend to believe, at times as if it were gospel, the so-called expert information generated by computers. He cites clear historical examples as a warning of what may come. Postman strongly suggests that as a culture dependent on technology, we must take steps now to objectively evaluate the past and present frenzy over and uncritical use of technology. He advises that we put technology in an appropriate perspective within our culture so that in the future we are not defined and controlled by it.

In introducing the concept of *Technopoly,* Postman begins with a philosophical lesson from Plato's Phaedrus and the story of King Thamus. Briefly, Thamus is concerned about the invention of writing and the effect that it will have on individual wisdom and memory. He foresees the invention of writing as damaging because the technology it provides by means of the written form will eliminate the need for memory. According to Thamus, wisdom will be lost because students will reference written information rather than their memories and they will not have a deep enough or sufficient appreciation or understanding of the knowledge they have gained. Thamus fails to see the positive benefits provided by writing as a technology—for example, the precise preservation of historical facts and records.

Postman draws on a wide range of sources for his interpretation. Fundamentally, he is concerned with the question of how new technology can most appropriately be used. Although he clearly recognizes that technologies such as the computer are not neutral, but instead value laden, he does not ground his work in the existing literature on computers and education and culture. There is no mention in his work, for example, of studies such as C. A. Bowers *The Cultural Meaning of Educational Computing* (1988) or E. F. Provenzo, Jr.'s *Beyond the Guteneberg Galaxy: Microcomputers and the Emergence of Post-Typographic Culture* (1986). In this sense, Postman is perhaps something of a computer illiterate.

One of the most disturbing concepts in Technopoly is the use of technology to control other technology that is employed to direct human behavior.

In the final chapter, "The Loving Resistance Fighter," Postman states his belief that the educational system within the United States must serve as the catalyst for change. Additionally, he asserts that schools have to go back to basics—what should be taught throughout the curriculum is the history of subjects, semantics, philosophy, comparative religion, and critical thinking. This, as Postman states, "will help to begin and sustain a serious conversation that will allow us to distance ourselves from that (technological) thought-world, and then criticize and modify it" (199). His argument has some merit, especially when applied as an opportunity to evaluate the effectiveness of technology on culture and the direction our society is headed. Throughout his book, he considers the negative and frightening effects of technology without any discourse on the benefits or positive aspects.

Postman points out in the first chapter the nonneutrality of technology, equity issues surrounding the accessibility of technology, and how the advent of technological progress redefines knowledge, vocabulary, religion, and culture. He expounds on the fact that historically schools have been oblivious to the technological takeover. Technology, specifically the computer, should be used as a learning tool. Instead, it is changing conceptions of how learning is to take place and what should be learned.

Chapters 2 and 3 take us through time, providing a background in the concepts and definitions of tool-using cultures, technocracy, and the culture of Technopoly. Postman explains technology in the tool-using culture as having two purposes: one is to solve specific challenges and meet day-to-day basic needs, as in waterpower, windmills, and the heavy-wheeled plow. The second purpose for tools is symbolic such as in art, politics, myth, ritual, and in religion, as in the painting of the Last Supper, cathedrals, and castles. He also states that technology used as tools did not intrude on or direct the culture but was an unassuming part of the religion and traditions of the society. During this period, before the European Middle Ages, theology was driving society. What was important, what was proper, and what was acceptable, was dictated by the church.

In the midst of the European Middle Ages, technology was beginning to make inroads into the "thought-world" of the culture. Tools were no longer simply integrated into the culture, they were changing the meaning of culture. For example, the mechanical clock originally devised as a tool to mark time for religious observances was changed into an instrument of commercial enterprise. In 1370 King Charles V ordered the citizens of Paris to organize all parts of their lives —social, work, and religious—by the bells of the royal palace clock (which struck every sixty minutes), thus significantly changing the concept of order.

It is paradoxical that men such as Copernicus, Galileo, and Descartes among others, who influenced the change from a tool-using culture to a technocracy, were all devoutly religious, and yet their work undermined the church's power. There were 200 years of cultural change before Technocracy's influence was readily recognized. By 1776 Technocracy had reshaped the concepts of culture and defined it, as Postman puts it, "as a society only loosely controlled by social custom and religious tradition and driven by the impulse to invent" (41). In the nineteenth century, invention was not a necessity as it was in the Middle Ages. Invention was now motivated by the perceived control the inventor gained in the act of inventing. In reality, according to Postman, traditional control was lost to technological control.

With the industrial revolution in the United States so came the era of Technopoly. Again, definitions of culture, tradition, religion, and politics changed as did concepts of truth, wisdom, and justice. Technology had begun to impose a form of government in which the political authority it exercises creates absolute and centralized control over all aspects of life. The individual was subordinated to the technology, and opposition to political and cultural expression was suppressed. Postman gives four reasons for the emergence of Technopoly in the United States: "American character; the genius and audacity of American capitalists; the success of twentieth-century technology; and the loss of confidence in our belief systems and therefore in ourselves" (53–56).

Chapters 4 and 5 cover in depth what Postman calls *Technopoly:* the overavailability of information continually created by technology. According to Postman, the drive within individuals to access that information has resulted in elevating the mere existence of data to a metaphysical status. However, even with the use of extensive technology, there is no way to contain, categorize, and organize the massive quantities of information so that it can be of collective use, and thus it has become a divine mystery that has captured our faith. Because of this, our culture yields to science (i.e., if there has been a study on it or if a scientist says it is so, then we believe it).

Because there is no way to effectively manage the immense quantity of knowledge known as data, there is a breakdown of our defense schemas and the experts are called in to help us make sense of all the information. So-called experts control only pieces of the vast amounts of information, each claiming supremacy over social, psychological, and moral affairs as well as the technical affairs for their piece of the proverbial pie. They dole out only information that they believe we need. Postman notes that even within the curriculum of schools, control is maintained by legitimizing and discrediting certain information. The masses of humanity become ruled not by what information is available but by what information is being withheld by the experts.

Postman describes three technical methods that control the American Technopoly by withholding information: bureaucracy (which includes schools), expertise, and technical machinery (mostly in the form of the computer).

The next two chapters deal with the ideology of machines in medical technology and in computer technology. Indisputably, Postman argues the success of technology in the field of medicine; however, the use of that technology is neither neutral nor equitable. Computers can be found in or used with almost every form of technology, including the field of medicine. Postman boldly states that people accept explanations that begin with the words "The computer shows ..." or " The computer has determined. ..." This phrase, according to Postman, is Technopoly's equivalent of the statement "It is God's will" and he finds the effect is roughly the same (115). He goes on to explain that the deity of our era has become the computer, a nonneutral, nonequitable piece of equipment into which we have put not only our faith and belief but also our means for existing.

Because the computer can manipulate complex statistical information quickly, the experts use the computer to manipulate data to provide information that is acceptable to the public. If we do not like the outcome one way, the data is rerun through the computer to retrieve the information differently. It is the speed with which the computer manipulates complex data that consigns us to quickly accept it. Postman, in the chapter on scientism and the manipulation of data, explains that there are three interrelated ideas that allow this to happen: (1) human behavior described in terms of natural sciences, (2) organization of society on a rational and humane basis, and (3) the meaning for life found in indiscriminate faith in science.

In the chapter "The Great Symbol Drain," Postman contends that "somewhere near the core of Technopoly is a vast industry with license to use all available symbols to further the interests of commerce, by devouring the psyches of consumers" (170). Here he is showing how the principles of Technopoly in our consumable world are reshaping our minds and changing our culture. We believe so deeply in what is thrust upon us by media that the original meanings for the symbols of our society no longer have any significance. As an example, Postman cites the commercial for Hebrew National Frankfurters: They have to answer to a higher authority— God. This, according to Postman, trivializes religion as a cultural symbol. He also contends that education has been trivialized by the President's Commission Report, *A Nation at Risk* (1983), to the point of being little more than "an instrument of economic policy" (174).

In the final chapter, Postman contends that education is "America's principal instrument for correcting mistakes and for addressing problems that mystify and paralyze other social institutions" (185). He insists that technology should never be accepted as a part of the natural order of things. Education, in his mind, must go back to its philosophical and historical roots from kindergarten through college so that the past can be evaluated, scrutinized, criticized, and used to unravel the forces of this technopolistic world objectively.

I found this book an interesting documentary of the transformation of society from a tool-using culture to a high-tech, incoherent Technopoly. What I found missing (as was missing in King Thamus's story) was a discussion on the benefits of this technology for society. Issues not addressed in the book include the Internet, the World Wide Web, hypertext, and hypermedia as well as a discussion on the inherent risks and benefits of the information available through this media and a foreshadowing of what might come to be if we do not control them. Postman does not touch upon the creation of computer-simulated and virtual realities or how this technology will again change the structure and meaning of culture and society. Could it be that he is not aware of these technologies and thus ill prepared for these discussions? *Technopoly: The surrender of Culture to Technology* is nevertheless a thought-provoking narrative and conjures many thoughts about our future world. Postman raises several questions: For what purpose was the technology devised? Will it serve that purpose or another? How will it be controlled? Postman asserts that the catalyst for change will be in the schools. He further contends that curriculum, as nonneutral and inequitable as it is, must be such that it develops critical minds that objectively evaluate the technology of the day and place it in an appropriate perspective for society before it is unconditionally embraced. Although his book does not provide the means to accomplish this task, it is worth every educator's time to read and reflect upon his ideas.

References

Bowers, C. A. 1988. *The Cultural Dimensions of Educational Computing: Understanding the Nonneutrality of Technology.* New York: Teachers College Press.

National Commission on Excellence in Education. 1983. *A Nation at Risk: The Imperative for Educational Reform.* A Report to the Nation and the Secretary of Education, United States Department of Education.

Plato, Phaedrus, and Letters VII and VIII. 1973. New York: Penguin.

Provenzo, Eugene F. 1986. *Beyond the Gutenberg Galaxy: Microcomputers and the Emergence of Post-Typographic Culture.* New York: Teachers College Press.

The Connected Family: Bridging the Digital Generation Gap. Seymour Papert. Atlanta: Longstreet Press, 1996. pp. 211.

LYDIA C. BARZA
University of Miami

How will the computer revolution affect children, families, and education? This is the main question that Seymour Papert addresses in *The Connected Family.* The computer as an educational technology is as relevant in the family setting as it is in the school.

The computer as a new educational technology has inspired both radically pessimistic and optimistic visions of the future. Some foresee bug-eyed student drones pushing keys in regimented unison. Yet others see an emancipated mass of elated students, eagerly freeing themselves of the shackles of rote learning and using their newfound liberty to digitally explore the world around them. Papert's vision clearly is commensurate with the latter.

The views expressed in *The Connected Family* follow a line of reasoning based on several assumptions. First, Papert contends that children are not sufficiently challenged in school. He suggests that some acting-out behaviors, learning difficulties, and lack of motivation children display in school can be attributed to the fact that they are just plain bored. Software programs intended for children's use are accused of embodying shallow characters and tedious drill activities. Examples are presented as evidence of this cult of monotony.

A second assumption is that the goal of schooling is to teach children about how to learn. Papert argues that the exploratory or constructivist style is more beneficial than setting out to teach something specific as traditional school lessons seek to do. One of the primary tasks of schooling should be to help children develop critical thinking skills as outlined by Dewey. Papert states, "The role of the teacher is to create conditions for invention rather than to provide ready-made knowledge" (45). He advocates learning by living and thinking in a culture versus learning by being told. A compromise between constructivist and instructionist views is suggested although Papert does not discuss how to accomplish this. The acceptance of the computer as a standard addition to a child's repertoire of home entertainment and school technologies will inevitably lead to educational reform. Papert observes that emphasis of the three R's will shift as access to knowledge changes, and he identifies schools, as well as the textbook industry, among the culprits that act against megachange in schools.

These ideas lead us to a central premise of Papert: Given that children are not sufficiently challenged and ought to be taught how to learn, the computer is an ideal medium. Papert admonishes that "observing children using technology reminds us that they can do more than we think" (4). Different learning styles may lend themselves well to the computer format because it is generally agreed that learning by doing is both meaningful and motivating. He contends that technological objects in the modern world are conceptually opaque but that programming will serve the role of demystifying them. Papert attacks the drill-and-practice approach and accuses it of being impractical, superficial, and boring. Literacy is necessary in the computer context as a means of control: one must read and write in order to use a computer. Therefore, children will be motivated to develop literacy behaviors because they want to control aspects of the computer program. Papert states that "we learn what we need to learn" (146).

Perhaps the most intriguing of Papert's beliefs is that children should design and create their own educational software. It is not good enough to simply use old methods of teaching and transfer them to computer format. For example, the process of learning Logo (a programming language developed by Papert) is basically akin to learning a foreign language. His suggested method of becoming fluent is to use the sadly underrated method of trial and error, emphasizing that this self-directed process will lead to greater comprehension. The reader is invited to sample several family computer projects in chapter 6, including MicroWorlds, on a CD-ROM included with the book.

The Connected Family is targeted toward an audience of parents and grandparents. Throughout the text there exists a spirit of empowerment. Papert challenges the notion that computers are "hard" and encourages parents to try and explore. He advises parents, "Sit down with them—don't be afraid to get near the machine, the kid will protect you—and let them show you something they made or something they can do" (92). Parents and teachers do not have to be the authorities on everything, including computers, in order to teach effectively. Valuable shared learning experiences may be fostered through computer games, programming, and Internet surfing. He also advises that children who are not drawn to computers may see their use in narrow ways and may be in revolt against adults who force a computer on them.

Current parent worries about computers are similar to those expressed about television in the 1950s. Among the main worries is that children will grow up with a false sense of reality. Papert emphasizes that parents must be accountable for unfavorable influences by monitoring the quantity and quality of computer use. He strongly suggests that parents become involved in the computer policies of schools their children attend and, again, underscores the idea that one need not be a computer expert to do so. Characteristics of good and bad software are discussed as a guide for parents. The software industry is criticized for designing what seems marketable to parents rather than what will enrich children's actual learning experiences.

In this book, Papert provides some background knowledge and a review for parents and grandparents on the topic of how they can enhance learning through the computer, specifically programming and the Internet. He touches upon many facets of this topic without much specificity in any one area. The message inherent in Papert's work is that the computer is truly a children's machine. Thus, children should be the ones in control in order to maximize its potential and theirs.

Hyper/Text/Theory. George P. Landow (ed.). Baltimore: Johns Hopkins University Press, 1994. pp. 377.

KEITH GRAZIADEI
University of Miami

Philosophy, democratization, narratives, and hypertext are just some of the topics addressed in George P. Landow's *Hyper/Text/Theory*. Hypertext, according to Landow is characterized by "its combination of blocks of text joined by electronic links, for this combination emphasizes multiple connections rather than linear reading or organization" (Landow 1989). Hypertext has its origins in the 1940s in the work of Vannevar Bush, whose concept of a Memex machine—a "sort of mechanized private file and library"—was intended to aid researchers and scientists in organizing complex ideas and research topics (68). Subsequent work by Theodor Nelson (who coined the word *hypertext* in 1965) and Douglas Engelbart (the inventor of the computer mouse and icon interfaces for computers) paved the way for contemporary scholarly discussion of hypertext and its affect on contemporary literacy.

Hypertext theory has been a field predominantly explored by critical literary theorists. Theories of hypertext (and the essays in this work) draw on the ideas of not only critical literary theory but also on postmodernist and poststructuralist thought. Because hypertext has the potential to deconstruct text and challenge its authority, issues of power, equity, and access are particularly relevant to its discussion. A broad philosophical net is cast in the work. Thinkers such as Plato and Aristotle are visited in terms of their ideas of justice. The experiences of Ludwig Wittgenstein (1953, *Philosophical Investigations*) provide discussion points for hypertext theory as well. Michel de Certeaus (1983, *Practice of Everyday Life*) is referenced as well in the context of the metaphor of mapping and hypertext.

The significance of hypertext theory should not be underemphasized as it has direct implications for the field of educational foundations. As a manifestation of the new literacy that is emerging in contemporary society, such pedagogical functions as reading, writing, and communicating will be redefined. As hypertext and hypermedia (hypertext with sound, animation, etc.) become more widespread through our culture and educational system, readers and writers will transform or metamorphose themselves into what Landow terms *wreaders* (i.e., writer/readers). This networked textuality ultimately redefines literacy.

The essays and articles found in *Hyper/Text/Theory* make frequent reference to the contemporary groundbreaking electronic hypertext fictional work of Michael Joyce (1990, *Afternoon*), and the nonelectronic hypertext of Raymond Queneau's (1961) *Cent Mille Milliards de Poemes*. Of particular interest is the examination of "closure in narrative" discussed within the framework of Michael Joyce's *Afternoon*. Authors in *Hyper/Text/Theory* like J. Yellowlees Douglas make clear that hypertext models have existed in textual works long before their introduction in computer-based formats. James Joyce's (1939) *Finnegan's Wake* and William Burroughs's (1959) *Naked Lunch,* for example, provide clear historical antecedents in text-based literature to electronic hypertexts.

Hypertext works such as Joyce's *Afternoon* provide the material for much of the analysis provided by George Landow and his fellow contributors in *Hyper/Text/Theory*. Landow divides the book's articles into three main sections that include "Nonlinearity," "The Politics of Hyptertext," and "The New Writing.". The essays and articles gathered in *Hyper/Text/Theory* represent a wide perspective regarding the issues surrounding hypertext theory. Working through the concepts and arguments found in this collection of essays provides an effective theoretical framework for anyone interested in the general issues surrounding hypertext theory.

"What's a Critic to Do: Critical Theory in the Age of Hypertext" by Landow is the first of a series of discussions on electronic textuality. In this essay, Landow examines issues of change brought about by computer-mediated hypertext sys-

tems. He provides an acute analysis of hypertext systems, including their characteristics of multivocality, open-endedness, multilinear organization, and the
reconfiguration of hypertext. Included within this analysis is a description of dif-
fering hypertext systems involving stand-alone versus networked systems and
read-only versus read/write systems. Landow's cry of "What's a Critic to do?" references the potential role that hypertext has on critical literary theory, including redefinition of the author–reader relationships (wreader) and the effect of hypertext
on scholarship. Landow summarizes his belief in this context with the contention
that "the potent combination of the digital word and the electronic network fundamentally reconceives notions of scholarly communication" (13).

Landow also includes an examination of the misplaced concern many critics as-
cribe to hypertext generated by the view of "control feared ... by confusing increasingly old-fashioned centralized mainframe computing with the new
information technologies as a whole" (33). He closes this opening article by noting
that by examining the convergence of critical theory and hypertext technology, we
will gain a strong insight on "our present age of transition" (40).

In "Nonlinearity and Literary Theory," Espen J. Aarseth outlines a theory of
nonlinear texts and discusses the implications they may have on the practice of literary theory and criticism. Aarseth claims that text is more than what the reader
gets out of it and what the writer puts into it (59). With this as a guiding perspective, he moves into an analysis of nonlinearity, discussing such components as
determinability, transience, and movability. He discusses the "readerless text" in
his examination of Raymond Queneau's *Cent Mille Milliards de Poemes*. Aarseth
also discusses the current problems and challenges faced by the study of computer-mediated textualities. As he views it, "After the celebrated deaths of the author, the work, and reading, the text is now giving up the spirit...." (82).

Gunnar Liestol explores hypertext and narratives in "Wittgenstein, Genette,
and the Reader's Narrative in Hypertext" by discussing Ludwig Wittgenstein's explorations of hypertext in his *Philosophical Investigations*. Liestol examines
Wittgenstein's attempt to break free of linear reference while remaining con-
strained by the printed text and concludes that "hypertext reconfigures our way of
conceiving text" (87). Narrative exploration is also discussed by Liestol when he
investigates Gerard Genette's (1988) analysis of story and discourse. In particular,
the connection between the act of reading and duration is discussed. He also emphasizes the creation of "discourse as discoursed, as actually read" (97). Liestol focuses on the affect of hypertext, agreeing with Walter J. Ong's claim that
electronic culture creates a second orality (102). He believes that hypermedia is a
pronounced receiver medium in which the efficiency of communication is de-
creased (111). These ideas all lead to his belief that hypermedia "creates new conditions for experiencing information and meaning" (116).

"The Screener's Map: Michel de Certeaus's 'Wandersmanner' and Paul
Auster's Hypertextual Detective" by Mirelle Rosello is an investigation of the in-

terrelated qualities of reading and mapping. Rosello examines the relationship between body and text and also examines body and space. As Rosello points out, "There are basically two ways of appropriating space: one may either trace a path where none existed before or use an already constituted map" (129). Rosello claims we need to change our "perception of how the body and space relate to each other" (131). He proposes that the writer and reader converge as a *screener*, a traveler who neither uses nor creates maps. Rosello uses Michel de Certeaus's *Practice of Everyday Life* to elaborate on his conceptions of how bodies should relate to space, and in particular, within a hypertext environment. In essence, the "browser-wanderer" (Rosello's term) creates the text. Ultimately, he believes that we should view hypertexts "as the extraordinary complex mixture of randomness and organization, unpredictability and meaningfulness displaced by fractal images" (117).

J. Yellowlees Douglas presents a discussion on achieving closure in interactive narratives in his essay entitled, "'How do I Stop this Thing?': Closure and Indeterminacy in Interactive Narratives." He asks the fundamental question "Is closure what we search for in narratives?" (159). Douglas reaches the conclusion that when our expectations are violated (not affirmed), we, as readers, call on our understanding of the narrative structure as a guide. He believes that we navigate through what he calls "interactives" with the same goal as printed text even when we know the text will not validate or negate our predictions (184). He argues that our sense of closure is "satisfied when we manage to resolve narrative tensions and to minimize ambiguities, to explain puzzles, and to incorporate as many of the narrative elements as possible into a coherent problem" (185).

Terence Harpold in his essay "Conclusions" agrees with Douglas that hypertexts have a unique paradigm of narrative closure: "You can just stop reading, decide that you've had enough. But you cannot come to a definitive ending. ..." (193). By looking for closure in hypertext, the reader will subvert or give oneself up to the text (194). Harpold continues by adding that a blurring between primary text and *paratext,* as Landow would agree, is created by the lack of textual cues. He asserts that there is a loss of identity while reading the text. "The hypertext reader reads the text as would an obsessional, insofar as he believes the link" (209).

Hyper/Text/Theory shifts gears at this point as the articles move into a discussion of the politics of hypertext. Charles Ess opens this section with "The Political Computer: Hypertext, Democracy, and Habermas." In this essay, Ess sets out to provide support to the claim that the technologies of hypertext and computer communication will democratize communication and society (225). Through an analysis of Jurgen Habermas's (1990) theory of Communicative Action, Ess lays down the theoretical framework in support of the democratization claim. He philosophically argues that democracy and our desire for it is based on a universal claim. With Habermas's (1990) Discourse Ethics as a guide, Ess moves through his argument debunking postmodernist and poststructuralist foundations of hypertext as inadequate to meet the requirements of democratization (248). With a hypertext system based on Habermas's communicative ethics, he argues that democratization is a reality "since it [communicative ethics] provides a framework that both endorses and refines existing conceptions and observations regarding hypertext, networks, and democratic communication" (293).

"Physics and Hypertext; Liberation and Complicity in Art and Pedagogy" is Martin E. Rosenberg's discourse on the politics and validity of tropes in hypertext. Rosenberg focuses his discussion on the idea that the use of physics metaphors in hypertext is constraining (270). Of notable interest is Rosenberg's comparison of hypertext links to black/white holes in their ability to create disruptions and necessitate periods where the "traveler" or reader can adjust to the new system or "lexia." Rosenberg includes discussions on the use of hypertext in avant-garde and pedagogical contexts that leads to the realization of "how entrapped we remain within our geometry that determines the frames of our awareness" even in hypertext environments (291).

Smooth space versus striated space occupies the arguments proposed by Stuart Moulthrop in "Rhizome and Resistance: Hypertext and the Dreams of a New Culture." In this essay, Moulthrop discusses Deleuze and Guattari's ideas of "a chaotically distributed network" (the rhizome) leading to his question of whether hypertext systems are domains of striated space (303). As Moulthrop states, "Hypertext will not liberate us from geometry, rationalist method" (316). He views hypertext and technologies like them not as ends in themselves but merely as transitions (317).

Hyper/Text/Theory concludes with a final section, "The New Writing," which includes two essays. David Kolb in "Socrates in the Labyrinth" wonders if we can "do philosophy using hypertext" (323). Kolb raises interesting points as he analyzes the fundamentals of philosophical argument in general and their potential fit with hypertext. Kolb asserts that a philosophical argument must follow a line however discontinuous it may be. In making this point, he cautions that hypertext narratives do not provide a strong enough and continuous line of reason and he believes that hypertext has limitations in lexia that are "too independent and relations that are too geometrical" (332).

Gregory Ulmer closes *Hyper/Text/Theory* with a piece entitled "The Miranda Warnings: An Experiment in Hyperrhetoric." Ulmer's article is a hypertextual collection where there are "no set rules but a distributed memory" (346). Ulmer weaves concepts and ideas together in a metaphorical tapestry where access to information and truth are likened to the third degree and dancing the samba. He agrees with Seymour Papert that what is crucial to pedagogy is "understanding the recasting of knowledge into new forms" (352). Ulmer fluctuates between Carmen Miranda, Turing, Wittgenstein, Brazil, and a myriad of other dynamic concepts, places, and people. Ulmer adds that "the purpose of my experiment is not to play the imitation game straight, nor to leave the Turing test intact, but to devise a replacement for it, based on something having to do with the samba as the metaphor for an electronic relationship to information" (366).

As computer technologies continue to affect all aspects of our daily lives, a continued examination of how they mediate our literacy is crucial. The blurring of edges (as Landow terms it) between reader and writer creates fuzzier notions of the fundamental issues of authorship. We are becoming a networked collection of ideas, thoughts, and dreams, and as this continual group consciousness evolves, so to must our understanding of hypertext theory. Therefore, hypertext theory can no longer remain just the scholarly concern of critical literary theorists and philosophers. As our pathways converge within the technological horizon, pedagogical disciplines must begin to cross borders into this rapidly evolving system of electronic culture and literacy.

References

Burroughs, W. 1959. *Naked Lunch.*New York: Grove Weidenfeld.
De Certeaus, M. 1983. *The Practice of Everyday Life.* Berkeley: University of California Press.
Genette, G. 1988. *Narrative Discourse.* Ithaca, N.Y.: Cornell University Press.
Joyce, J. 1939. *Finnegan's Wake.* New York: Viking.
Joyce, M. 1990. *Afternoon: A Story.* Cambridge, Mass.: Eastgate Systems.
Landow, George P. 1989. "The Rhetoric of Hypermedia: Some Rules for Authors." *Journal of Computing in Higher Education* 1 (Spring): 39.
Queneau, R. 1961. *Cent Mille Milliards de Poemes.* Paris: Gallimard.
Wittgenstein, L. 1953. *Philosophical Investigations.* Oxford, England: Basil Blackwell.

The Cultural Dimensions of Educational Computing: Understanding the Non-Neutrality of Educational Computing. C. A. Bowers. New York: Teachers College Press, 1988. pp. v, 153.

MICHELE C. MITS CASH
University of Miami

In *The Cultural Dimensions of Educational Computing: Understanding the Non-Neutrality of Educational Computing,* C. A. Bowers addresses the use of the computer as a "transforming force" in education. Its importance for him, however, is largely "as an educational tool rather than as a technology that dictates the patterns of learning and social interaction" (1). Bowers's comments were made over a decade ago in 1988 and are all the more interesting considering what has transpired in the field of educational computing during the decade of the 1990s.

Bowers argued in 1988 that the technological experts who design hardware and software applications do not address educational issues. Instead they are concerned primarily with programming and procedures that manipulate the calculating and information-processing power of the machine while mostly ignoring the larger social and cultural issues that are critical to the use of the technology in educational settings. Bowers objects to the fact that educational computing is largely decontextualized as a result of the "practice of segmenting experience into discrete components and of thinking that expertise is acquired by learning about and technologically mastering that component part. The problem with this form of thinking is that it fails to recognize that the discrete entities we isolate for study are an integral part of a complex ecology that includes both the cultural and natural environment" (2). Bowers also addresses the frightening concept of the Panopticon Society where individuals are under constant surveillance. He relates that educators must consider seriously the cultural orientation that is being reinforced in the classroom—in the use of computers to collect and collate details on test scores, reading habits, and administrative functions as well as the further capacity for close surveillance of individual activity.

Throughout the book, Bowers brings to the forefront many important questions regarding the appropriate use of microcomputers in educational settings. The most fundamental question found in the book is addressed in chapter 2 and concerns the non-neutrality of computers and educational software. Bowers frames this concern by asking, "Is the technology (in the form of the microcomputer) neutral in terms of accurately representing, at the level of the software program, the domains of the real world in which people live?" (24). He finds Robert Taylor's (1980) concept of computer as tutor, tool, and tutee an inappropriate model that reinforces the notion of neutrality. Likewise, he laments what he believes are Seymour Papert's cultural misconceptions regarding the autonomous nature of the individual and the rational process. Bowers argues strongly that when language is combined with technology, it mediates students' understanding of the ecological environment in which they live.

A critically important point within Bower's book is Don Ihde's (1979) conceptual notion of *amplification* and *reduction,* which can briefly be defined as the belief that technology transforms our experiences by selectively augmenting certain aspects of experience and by diminishing others. An example of this idea provided by Ihde explores how "the telephone can be seen as amplifying our voice over distance while simultaneously reducing our ability to use our own or the other person's body language (completely eliminating the visual, tactile, and olfactory dimensions of the experience)" (Ihde 1979, 56). Bowers takes this idea and transfers it to the computer, asking the fundamental question, What is it that a technology-like educational computing selects for amplification and reduction? To answer his question, Bowers evaluates educational programs such as *The Oregon Trail,* Papert's programming language Logo, and Apple's school-based educational program the *Classroom of Tomorrow.*

Bowers suggests that the computer amplifies or encourages the misconception of data being completely objective and reduces the experience of tacit-heuristic forms of knowledge that actually underlie experience. He further suggests that the computer reduces the students' awareness that data, in the form of the program, is an interpretation and selection of information collected by the programmer—who brings his own experiences and perspectives to the construction of the program. Students with limited experience take what the programmer has created as being absolute rather than relative. In the process, the true meaning of what is being taught and transferred through the software is potentially distorted.

Because the microcomputer mediates the students' experience with culture via its program, or language code, it cannot be separated from the concept of language socialization. Bowers asserts that students interacting with microcomputers are involved in a process of communication that is influenced by cultural assumptions and language-thought processes that are an integral part of the person who wrote the software. The control of language then influences the students' ability to recognize and decipher certain forms of information that emerge from the material being studied. He maintains that another result of amplification and reduction of cultural information is the fact that it is almost universally accepted that students must be computer literate to participate fully in our information-based society.

According to Bowers, one cultural aspect that has come to be in direct competition with the non-neutrality of the microcomputer are the thought processes and social relationships associated with the oral tradition. In Bowers's discussion of the research of Walter Ong (1977, 1982), Ronald and Suzanne Scollon (1985), and Sylvia Scribner and Michael Cole (1981), he notes that education, starting with the Renaissance, has advocated literacy over orality—assuming that the written word is a more reliable source of knowledge. Oral communication depends heavily upon the use of visual context and paralinguistic signals as part of the message exchange. Writing involves a fixed text, with visual and tactile sensory input allowing for analysis between different compositions. The power of print is in the amplification of the autonomous sense of individualism and analytical thought. In this context, the microcomputer acts as extension of the autonomous nature of writing. According to Bowers, critical issues to consider are how students are socialized and how well prepared teachers are to make professional judgments. He further asserts the need to "understand the differences between the written and spoken word to help us recognize deeper issues that must be addressed when deciding how educational computing fits within the cultural transmission process in the classroom, as well as when its use with minority cultural groups becomes a disguised form of cultural domination" (79).

Chapter 4 is a discussion of "the teacher's responsibility for the recovery of the symbolic world." Bowers suggests that few teachers and educational computing experts have made the connection between computer technology, cultural ideology and politics, leading students to believe that the information age is simply defined by access and use of the computer. He asserts that there has been an "acceptance of the assumption that individuals must be prepared to process massive amounts of information if they are to make rational decisions. This assumption about autonomous individuals faced with a many-layered world of data makes the computer appear to be a latter-day Promethean gift, as basic to the continuation of the social existence as the original gift of fire" (88). Bowers sees another missed connection in the form of collective memory and gender bias. He frames the problem as a lack of understanding between educational computing and male gender dominance over basic cultural thinking. This is ironic because, as he points out, women tend to have a better understanding of the importance of relations in the giving and receiving of information during the process of communication and problem solving than men. In this context, it is clear that computer technology is not gender neutral.

Cultural literacy, in the form of consciousness-raising and primary socialization, is, according to Bowers, the teacher's responsibility in the educational process. He believes that classrooms should be viewed as being ecologically part of a complex language process whereby teachers are passing on to the students through the appropriate use of technology (writing, speaking, computing) cultural patterns, norms, and procedures for thinking and interacting with others. He further suggests that educational computing does not take away or change the teacher's responsibility for providing the symbolic foundation necessary for an informed and critically reflective mode of thinking. Bowers warns that teachers and educational-computing experts must recognize that the important issues to be addressed in educational computing are the nontechnical educational issues (effects of cultural literacy, not computer literacy).

In his final chapter, "Educational Computing in Third World Countries: A Restatement of Themes," Bowers focuses on the desire of third-world countries to modernize with computer technology. The problem, as Bowers sees it, is that these cultures continue to view computer technology as being culturally neutral and having the ability to contribute to a nondependent form of social development. It is unrealistic, he contends, to introduce educational computing on the assumption that it is adaptable to the local culture simply by changing the content of the instructional software program. What is not understood is that local traditions are disturbed and disrupted by the technology and the established culture ceases to be part of the ongoing patterns of everyday life in these developing countries.

In *The Cultural Dimensions of Educational Computing* Bowers raises many important and thought-provoking questions—ones that every educator and educational-technology expert should consider before integrating the use of microcomputers and educational software into their curriculum. Much of his discourse is focused on issues relating to the question of defining cultural literacy versus computer literacy and how each can best be developed from a pedagogical perspective. Questions of amplification and reduction of materials and historical facts, as well as who determines what will be taught, are thoroughly explored. How the educator uses technology, especially in the form of the microcomputer in the classroom, is of paramount importance if we are to have a society of thinkers or conversely a society of individuals who merely interpret data collected by someone else. Bowers encourages further research based in educational, sociological, and philosophical contexts. In doing so, he makes a seminal contribution to understanding computers in both our culture and curriculum.

References

Ihde, Don. 1979. *Technics and Praxis*. Dordrecht, Holland: D. Reidel.
Ong, Walter J. 1977. *Interfaces of the Word: Studies in the Evolution of Consciousness and Culture*. Ithaca, N.Y.: Cornell University Press.
―――. 1982. *Orality and Literacy: The Technologizing of the Word*. London and New York: Methuen.
Scollon, Ronald, and Suzanne Scollon. 1985. *The Problem of Power*. Haines, Alaska: Gutenberg Dump.
Scribner, Sylvia, and Michael Cole. 1981. *The Psychology of Literacy*. Cambridge: Harvard University Press.
Taylor, Robert, ed. 1980. *The Computer in the Schools: Tutor, Tools, Tutee*. New York: Teachers College Press.

Computers as Theatre. Brenda Laurel. Reading, Mass.: Addison-Wesley, 1991. pp. 211.

AUBREY CAMPBELL
University of Miami

A twenty-year veteran of the entertainment software industry, Brenda Laurel has become known as a human–computer interface expert. Well known by many entertainment figures, Laurel has recently advocated greater involvement than mere interface design. She urged interface designers to expand their influence beyond traditional interface design boundaries to express humanistic values in terms of the form, structure, and purpose of software, especially in the entertainment business. It is my pleasure to review the ideas contained in her book, *Computers as Theatre*.

In chapter 1, Laurel maps a journey of concurrently creating and discovering simulated, participatory action through computer graphics, at the time (1991) a new medium competing with film animation. For Laurel, the computer's potential to represent participatory human action surpasses its ability to perform calculations. She sees the development of computers (Apple Macintosh) as depicting an "interface evolution" that allows more intimate human–computer interaction than previously possible. Laurel equates this human–computer interface to the drama–audience interface embodied in the title of her book. She thoroughly analyzes this interface metaphor and proposes a more complex one. She concludes this chapter with the view that human–computer interface design is about "creating imaginary worlds that have a special relationship to reality—worlds in which we can extend, amplify, and enrich our own capacities to think, feel, and act" (33).

Chapter 2 applies a dramatic theory framework to the art of designing human–computer experiences. Laurel argues for an understanding of the tools of the trade of creating plays and describes the concurrent, interactive forces that operate when creating dramatic plays. She links the causes of human–computer activity to the fundamental principles of creating dramatic art for and through the computer. Laurel recognizes the failures of human–computer activity as failures on the thought level because plays and human–computer activities alike are "closed universes that delimit the set of potential actions" and thought (58).

Chapter 3 outlines the construction of *representational actions.* In this chapter, Laurel defines the characteristic elements of form and structure of dramatic action and relates these to human–computer activity. She makes the important point that each human–computer action—whether or not a game or task is completed—is a multitude of *whole actions,* each representing a dramatic play. Each computer session progresses from possibility, to probability, to action, to end. Each session at the computer contains all the elements of a standard play with beginning, middle, and end.

In Chapter 4, Laurel explores techniques of applying theoretical knowledge about dramatic art to the "task of designing interesting, engaging, and satisfying human–computer activities" (93). However, the constraints of the dramatic form of a play restrict its design, in the same way the constraints of a computer program restrict its design. This chapter further outlines the benefits of a dramatic approach to computer engagement and emotion and emphasizes the need to delimit and represent human–computer activities or interaction —"organic wholes with structural characteristics," as found in dramatic plays.

Chapter 5 describes design principles for human–computer activity according to Aristotle's observation that art is "not what is, but [art is] a kind of thing that might be" (125), that real life is represented within a broad spectrum of deviation from real life. Laurel argues that people prefer real-world objects because such objects are then cognitively less demanding. Real-world objects make representations more accessible and therefore more enjoyable to a larger audience. Because of their growing interactivity, computers have evolved into an increasingly representational medium. This mutual influence between interactivity and representation has seen rapid growth in both elements. Laurel describes this as Symmetry in Representation, which argues for cognitive congruence between the various modalities of computer simulation. For example, high-resolution animation associated with basic machine beeps creates cognitive dissonance in the human agent.

The human mind expects the elements of the computer "play" to work together at compatible, congruent cognitive levels. In the absence of this congruence, computer plays lose their authenticity, their realism.

With her concluding chapter, Laurel anticipates increased sophistication of both computer software and hardware. She predicts that increased sophistication will lead to increased natural human tasking integrated into whole action on the computer. Laurel also foresees that integrated environments of virtual reality present the possibility of "doing things that we simply couldn't do before" (169). The chapter further describes Laurel's personal computer environment, an experiment in which she explores the creation of possible human–computer plays within that virtual reality.

At the time of the publication of *Computers as Theatre,* Laurel's exploration of a computer-based playwriting and learning space was fresh and futuristic. She literally creates an environment conducive to creating computer plays, of creating human–computer interaction, of creating virtuality. In the subsequent years since the publication of her book, much of her philosophical constructs have matured and mellowed. However, the rapidly increasing dynamism of both computer hardware and software in recent years has seen most of what Laurel foretold come to fruition and become daily events. The computer's ability to represent and create new environments in which humans can learn, explore, and act, has blown a hole through which "cause and effect are a quantum leap in human evolution" (198) both on and off the stage of the computer theatre. The computer has indeed evolved and matured into a living space both on and off stage.

BOOKS AVAILABLE LIST

BOOKS RECEIVED FALL/WINTER 1999

Angus, David L., and Jeffrey E. Mirel. *The Failed Promise of the American High School, 1890–1995.* New York: Teachers College Press, 1999. pp. 259. $26.95 (paper).

Cherryholmes, Cleo H. *Reading Pragmatism.* New York: Teachers College Press, 1999. pp. 148. $24.95 (paper).

Crotty, Michael. *The Foundations of Social Research: Meaning and Perspective in the Research Process.* Thousand Oaks, Calif.: Sage, 1999. pp. 250. $21.95 (paper).

Cuban, Larry. *How Scholars Trumped Teachers: Change Without Reform in University Curriculum, Teaching, and Research, 1890–1990.* New York: Teachers College Press, 1999. pp. 275. $28.95 (paper).

Dixon, Kathleen, ed. *Outbursts in Academe: Multiculturalism and Other Sources of Conflict.* Westport, Conn.: Heinemann, 1999. pp. 179. $22.00 (paper).

Esposito, Virginia M., ed. *Conscience and Community: The Legacy of Paul Ylvisaker.* New York: Peter Lang Publishing, 1999. pp. 432. $34.95 (cloth).

Gabbard, David A., ed. *Knowledge and Power in the Global Economy: Politics and the Rhetoric of School Reform.* Mahwah, N.J.: Lawrence Erlbaum Associates, Inc., 2000. pp. 430. $39.95 (paper).

Gibboney, Richard A. *What Every Great Teacher Knows: Practical Principles for Effective Teaching.* Brandon, Vt.: Holistic Education Press, 1999. pp. 139. $18.95 (paper).

Kliebard, Herbert. *Schooled to Work: Vocationalism and the American Curriculum, 1876–1946.* New York: Teachers College Press, 1999. pp. 291. $22.95.

Kozulin, Alex. *Vygotsky's Psychology: A Biography of Ideas.* Cambridge: Harvard University Press, 1999. pp. 286. $19.95 (paper).

Lipkin, Arthur. *Understanding Homosexuality, Changing Schools: A Text for Teachers, Counselors, and Administrators.* Boulder, Colo.: Westview, 1999. pp. 483. $69.00 (cloth).

Massey, Alexander, and Geoffrey Wolford. *Studies in Educational Ethnography.* Vol. 2, *Explorations in Methodology.* Stamford, Conn.: JAI/Ablex, 1999. pp. 250. $78.50 (cloth).

McClellan, B. Edward. *Moral Education in America: Schools and the Shaping of Character from Colonial Times to the Present.* New York: Teachers College Press, 1999. pp. 130. $ 21.95 (paper).

Noblit, George W. *Particularities: Collected Essays on Ethnography and Education.* New York: Peter Lang, 1999. pp. 240. $29.95 (paper).

O'Brien, Thomas V. *Politics of Race and Schooling: Public Education in Georgia, 1900–1961.* Lanham, Mass.: Lexington Books, 1999. pp. 256. $45.00 (cloth).

Olessen, Mark. *Michel Foucault: Materialism and Education.* Westport, Conn.: Greenwood, 1999. pp. 216. $59.95 (cloth).

Peter, Michael, ed. *After the Disciplines: The Emergence of Cultural Studies.* Westport, Conn.: Greenwood, 1999. pp. 300. $69.50 (cloth).

Purdy, Jedediah. *For Common Things: Irony, Trust, and Commitment in America Today.* New York: Knopf, 1999. pp. 226. $20.00 (cloth).

Schultz, Lucille M. *The Young Composers: Composition's Beginnings in Nineteenth–Century Schools.* Carbondale, Ill.: Southern Illinois University Press, 1999. pp. 200.

Smith, David Geoffrey. *Interdisciplinary Essays in the Pedagon: Human Sciences, Pedagogy and Culture.* New York: Peter Lang, 1999. pp. 216. $29.95 (paper).

Speck, Bruce W., Teresa R. Johnson, Catherine P. Dice, and Leon B. Heaton. *Collaborative Writing: An Annotated Bibliography.* Westport, Conn.: Greenwood, 1999. pp. 408. $79.50 (cloth).

Wells, Gordan. *Diagnostic Inquiry: Towards A Sociocultural Practice and Theory of Education.* New York: Cambridge University Press, 1999. pp. 275. $64.95 (cloth).

Westbury, Ian, Stephan Hopman, and Kurt Riquarts. *Teaching as a Reflective Practice: The German Didactik Tradition.* Mahwah, N.J.: Lawrence Erlbaum Associates, Inc.: 2000. pp. 346. $69.95 (cloth).

Zevin, Jack. *Social Studies for the Twenty First Century: Methods and Materials for Teaching in Middle and Secondary Schools.* Mahwah, N.J.: Lawrence Erlbaum Associates, Inc., 1999. pp. 440. $49.95 (cloth).

BOOKS RECEIVED SPRING AND SUMMER 1999

Ahier, John, and Geoff Esland, eds. *Education, Training and the Future of Work I: Social, Political and Economic Contexts of Policy Development.* New York: Routledge, 1999. pp. 271. $25.99 (paper).

Allen, Lew. *A Guide to Renewing Your School.* San Francisco: Jossey-Bass, 1999. pp. xxii, 114. $28.95 (paper).

Amiram, Raviv, Louis Oppenheimer, and Daniel Bar-Tal, eds. *How Children Understand War and Peace: A Call for International Peace Education.* San Francisco: Jossey-Bass, 1999. pp. 342. $44.95 (cloth).

Appel, Stephen. *Psychoanalysis and Pedagogy.* Critical Studies in Education Series, edited by Henry A. Giroux. Westport, Conn.: Greenwood, 1999. pp. 208. $55.00 (cloth).

Berman, Jeffery. *Surviving Literacy Suicide.* Amherst: University of Massachusetts Press, 1999. pp. 290. $18.95 (paper).

Bigler, Ellen. *American Conversations: Puerto Ricans, White Ethics, and Multicultural Education.* Philadelphia: Temple University Press, 1999. pp. 289. $19.95 (paper).

Boyles, Deron. *American Education and Corporations: The Free Market Goes to School.* Levittown, Pa: Taylor & Francis, 1999. pp. 217. $60.00 (cloth).

Brookfield, Stephen D., and Stephen Preskill. *Discussion as a Way of Teaching: Tools and Techniques for Democratic Classrooms.* San Francisco: Jossey-Bass, 1999. pp. xx, 320. $32.95 (cloth).

Caulkins, Jonathan P., C. Peter Rydell, Susan S. Everingham, James Chiesa, and Shawn Bushway, eds. *An Ounce of Prevention, a Pound of Uncertainty: The Cost Effectiveness of School-Based Drug Prevention Programs.* Washington, D.C.: RAND, 1999. pp. 194. $15.00 (paper).

Darling-Hammond, Linda, and Gary Sykes, eds. *Teaching as the Learning Profession: Handbook of Policy and Practice.* San Francisco: Jossey-Bass, 1999. pp. 426. $49.95 (cloth).

Evans, Nancy J., Deanna S. Forney, and Florence Guido-DiBrito. *Student Development in College: Theory Research and Practice.* San Francisco: Jossey-Bass, 1998. pp. 320. $32.95 (cloth).

Harris, Margaret, and Giyoo Hatano, eds. *Learning to Read and Write: A Cross-Linguistic Perspective.* New York: Cambridge University Press. pp. 252. $59.95 (cloth).

Heath, Douglas H. *Morale, Culture, and Character: Assessing Schools of Hope.* Bryn Mawr, Penn.: Conrow, 1999. pp. 290.

Heath, Douglas H. *Assessing Schools of Hope: Methods, Norms, and Case Studies.* Bryn Mawr, Penn: Conrow, 1999. pp. 166.

Hefzallah, Ibrahim Michail. *The New Educational Technologies and Learning: Empowering Teachers to Teach and Students to Learn in the Information Age.* Springfield, Ill.: Charles C. Thomas, 1999. pp. 301. $62.95 (cloth).

Jelloun, Tahar Ben. *Racism Explained to My Daughter*. New York: The New Press, 1999. pp. 208. $16.95 (paper).

Kanpol, Barry. *Critical Pedagogy*. Westport, Conn.: Greenwood, 1999. pp. 224. $59.95 (paper).

Kincheloe, Joe L., Shirley R. Sternberg, and Leila E. Villaverde, eds. *Rethinking Intelligence: Confronting Psychological Assumptions About Teaching and Learning*. New York: Routledge, 1999. pp. 270. $22.99 (paper).

Labaree, David F. *How to Succeed in School: Without Really Learning*. New Haven, Conn.: Yale University Press, 1999. pp. 320. $18.00 (paper).

Milbrath, Constance. *Patterns of Artistic Development in Children: Comparative Studies of Talent*. New York: Cambridge University Press, 1998. pp. 422. $59.95 (cloth).

Mitchell, Bruce M., and Robert E. Salsbury. *Encyclopedia of Multicultural Education*. Westport, Conn.: Greenwood, 1999. pp. 305. $65.00 (cloth).

Morgan, Harry. *The Imagination of Early Childhood Education*. Westport, Conn.: Greenwood, 1999. pp. 272. $59.95 (cloth).

Purpel, David E. *Moral Outrage in Education*. New York: Peter Lang, 1999. pp. 257. $29.95 (paper).

Raelin, Joseph A. *Work-Based Learning: The New Frontier of Management Development*. Upper Saddle River, N.J.: Prentice Hall, 1999. pp. 279.

Sheets, Rosa Hernandez, and Etta R. Hollins. *Racial and Ethnic Identity in School Practices: Aspects of Human Development*. Mahwah, N.J.: Lawrence Erlbaum Associates, Inc., 1999. pp. ix, 271. $27.50 (paper), $59.50 (cloth).

Sidorkin, Alexander M. *Beyond Discourse: Education, the Self, and Dialogue*. Albany: State University of New York Press, 1999. pp. 150. $15.95 (paper).

Sirotnik, Kenneth A., and Roger Soder, eds. *The Beat of a Different Drummer: Essays on Educational Renewal in Honor of John I. Goodlad*. New York: Peter Lang, 1999. pp. 336. $35.95 (cloth).

Smith, Wilma F., and Gary D. Fenstermacher, eds. *Leadership for Educational Renewal: Developing a Cadre of Leaders*. Agenda for Education in a Democracy Series, edited by Timothy J. McMannon. San Francisco: Jossey-Bass, 1999. pp. 400. $29.95 (paper).

Schneider, Barbara, and David Stevenson. *The Ambitious Generation: America's Teenagers Motivated but Directionless*. New Haven, Conn.: Yale University Press, 1999. pp. 321. $26.00 (cloth).

Spitz, Ellen Handler. *Inside Picture Books*. New Haven, Conn.: Yale University Press, 1999. pp. 230. $25.00 (cloth).

Symes, Colin, and Daphne Meadmore. *The Extraordinary School: Parergonality and Pedagogy*. New York: Peter Lang, 1999. pp. 212. $29.95 (paper).

Thayer-Bacon, Barbara J., and Charles S. Bacon. *Philosophy Applied to Education: Nurturing a Democratic Community in the Classroom*. Columbus, OH: Merrill, 1999. pp. 235.

Tierney, William G. *Building the Responsive Campus: Creating High Performance Colleges and Universities*. Thousand Oaks, CA: Sage, 1999. pp. 185. $21.95 (paper).

Waxler, Robert P., and Jean R. Troustine, eds. *Changing Lives Through Literature*. Notre Dame: The University of Notre Dame Press, 1999. pp. 342.

Zuss, Mark. *Subject Present: Life-Writings and Strategies of Representation*. New York: Peter Lang, 1999. pp. 262. No price listed (paper).

BOOKS RECEIVED WINTER 1999

Brunner, C. Cryss, ed. *Sacred Dreams: Women and the Superintendency*. Albany: State University of New York Press, 1999. pp. xvi, 231. $18.95 (paper).

Clark, Christine, and James O'Donnell. *Becoming and Unbecoming White: Owning and Disowning a Racial Identity*. Westport, Conn.: Bergin & Garvey, 1999. pp. xiii, 283.

Coulson, Andrew J. *Market Education: The Unknown History*. New Brunswick, N.J.: Social Philosophy and Policy Center, Transaction Publishers, 1999. pp. x, 470. $24.95 (paper).

Feinberg, Walter. *Common Schools/Uncommon Identities: National Unity and Cultural Difference*. New Haven, Conn.: Yale University Press, 1998. pp. x, 264. $28.50 (cloth).

Heinz, Walter R., ed. *From Education to Work: Cross-National Perspectives*. Cambridge: Cambridge University Press, 1999. pp. x, 352. $59.95 (cloth).

Hollins, Etta R., and Eileen I. Oliver, ed. *Pathways to Success in School: Culturally Responsive Teaching*. Mahwah, N.J.: Lawrence Erlbaum Associates, Inc. 1999. pp. xvi, 211. $24.50 (paper).

Murphy, Joseph, Scott W. Gilmer, Richard Weise, and Ann Page. *Pathways to Privatization in Education*. Greenwich, Conn.: Ablex, 1998. pp. xiii, 244. $73.25 (Cloth), $24.95 (paper).

Nardi, Bonnie A., and Vicki L. O'Day. *Information Ecologies: Using Technology with Heart*. Cambridge: MIT Press, 1999. pp. xiv, 232. $27.50 (cloth).

Nash, Robert J. *Faith, Hype, and Clarity: Teaching About Religion in American Schools and Colleges*. New York: Teachers College Press, 1999. pp. x, 214. $51.00 (cloth), $23.95 (paper).

Paley, Vivian Gussin. *The Kindness of Children*. Cambridge, MA: Harvard University Press, 1999. pp. 129. $18.95 (cloth).

Ravitch, Diane, ed. *Brookings Papers on Education Policy*. Washington D.C.: Brookings Institution Press, 1999. pp. 462. $19.95 (paper).

Reed, Ronald F., and Tony W. Johnson. *Friendship and Moral Education: Twin Pillars of Philosophy for Children*. New York: Peter Lang, 1999. pp. 227. $29.95 (paper).

Spangler, Mary Michael. *Aristotle on Teaching*. Lanham, Md.: University Press of America, 1998. pp. ix, 234. $49.00 (cloth), $29.50 (paper).

Taylor, Todd, and Irene Ward. *Literacy Theory in the Age of the Internet*. New York: Columbia University Press, 1998. pp. xxi, 177. $47.50 (cloth), $17.50 (paper).

BOOKS RECEIVED FALL 1998

Blades, David W. *Procedures of Power and Curriculum Change: Foucault and the Quest for Possibilities in Science Education*. New York: Peter Lang, 1997. pp. xii, 290.

Cohen, Arthur M. *The Shaping of American Higher Education: Emergence and Growth of the Contemporary System*. San Francisco: Jossey-Bass, 1998. pp. xiii, 495. $39.95 (cloth).

Cardozier, V. R. *University of Texas Permian Basin: A History*. Austin, Tex.: Eakin Press, 1998. pp. vii, 280. $19.95 (paper).

Currie, Jan, and Janice Newson. *Universities and Globalization*. Thousand Oaks, Calif.: Sage, 1998. pp. xii, 339. $29.95 (paper).

Hoy, Terry. *The Political Philosophy of John Dewey: Towards a Constructive Renewal*. Westport, Conn.: Praeger, 1998. pp. 141. $49.95 (cloth).

Mitchell, Samuel. *Reforming Educators: Teachers, Experts, and Advocates*. Westport, Conn.: Praeger, 1998. pp. 261. $59.95 (cloth).

Neilsen, Lorri. *Knowing Her Place: Research Literacies and Feminist Occasions*. San Francisco: Caddo Gap Press, 1998. pp. 288. $25.95 (paper).

Semali, Ladislaus, and Ann Watts Pailliotet, eds. *Intermediality: The Teachers' Handbook of Critical Media Literacy*. Boulder, Colo.: Westview, 1998. pp. ix, 238. $60.00 (cloth), $23.00 (paper).

Smith, M. Cecil, ed. *Literacy for the Twenty-First Century: Research, Policy, Practices, and the National Adult Literacy Survey*. Westport, Conn.: Praeger, 1998. pp. ix, 212. $59.95 (cloth).